SWIMMING
WITH FAITH

Milford Town Library
80 Spruce Street
Milford, MA 01757

Other Books in the Zonderkidz Biographies Series

SWIMMING
WITH FAITH

Natalie Davis Miller

The Missy Franklin Story

ZONDER**kidz**

ZONDERKIDZ

Swimming with Faith
Copyright © 2016 by Natalie Davis Miller

This title is also available as a Zondervan ebook.
Visit www.zondervan.com/ebooks

Requests for information should be addressed to:
Zonderkidz, 3900 Sparks Dr. SE, Grand Rapids, Michigan 49546

ISBN 978-0-310-74707-9

All scripture quotations, unless otherwise indicated, are taken from The Holy
Bible, New International Version®, NIV®. Copyright © 1973, 1978, 1984, 2011 by
Biblica, Inc.® Used by permission of Zondervan. All rights reserved worldwide.
www.zondervan.com. The "NIV" and "New International Version" are trademarks
registered in the United States Patent and Trademark Office by Biblica, Inc.®

Any Internet addresses (websites, blogs, etc.) and telephone numbers in this book
are offered as a resource. They are not intended in any way to be or imply an
endorsement by Zondervan, nor does Zondervan vouch for the content of these
sites and numbers for the life of this book.

All rights reserved. No part of this publication may be reproduced, stored in
a retrieval system, or transmitted in any form or by any means—electronic,
mechanical, photocopy, recording, or any other—except for brief quotations in
printed reviews, without the prior permission of the publisher.

Zonderkidz is a trademark of Zondervan.

Cover photo: ODD ANDERSON/AFP/Getty Images
Interior design: Denise Froehlich
Interior photo: istockphoto © Lee Regers

Printed in the United States of America

16 17 18 19 20 21 22 23 /DCI/ 15 14 13 12 11 10 9 8 7 6 5 4 3 2 1

For Aubrey, always an inspiration

Table of Contents

Chapter 1

Swims Like a Fish

Anyone might say that two years old is too young to swim in the ocean by yourself. But that didn't stop the little girl who would grow up to be arguably the greatest female athlete on the planet. When Missy Franklin was just two years old, her family went snorkeling in Maui. We know that it doesn't take much to get the attention of a small child and Missy was no different. A beautiful fish caught the toddler's eye and off she went, chasing after it and swimming away from shore. D.A. Franklin, Missy's mother, couldn't catch up to her. A scream from D.A. alerted Missy's father, Dick, who ran to the water after his little daughter.

According to an interview in *5280.com*, young Missy was in twelve feet of water, about thirty feet from shore. She was fast and she was fearless. And she got her parents' attention. Thankfully, Dick was able to catch up to her then, but he would be hard pressed to catch her now. In fact, there are few swimmers in the world who can catch or even keep up with this five-time Olympic medal winner.

It seems that all of her life Melissa "Missy" Franklin, much like a heat-seeking missile, has been pointed toward Olympic success. Even as a little girl who learned to swim at an early age, she drew pictures of the Olympic rings. When she was twelve years old she knew for sure that the Olympics would be a final destination. And with a body only God could make so perfectly for swimming, coupled with Missy's own tenacity, perseverance, and dedication to suit it, it is no wonder that a lifetime of preparation would lead to one inspiring summer where she would show the world what she was made of. The London 2012 Olympic Games had been waiting for Missy Franklin all of her life. Seven electrifying swimming events, four gold medals, and one bronze medal later, 17-year-old Missy Franklin let the world know that she had finally arrived.

Missy Franklin had always been fast. Swimming like a fish from an early age, the Olympic athlete with the infectious smile has held the world captive with her world-class talent and an unending happy disposition that could melt the coldest heart. At just 17 years old, Missy took the swimming world by storm when she qualified for a record seven events in the London 2012 Olympics. She followed that up by delivering on five Olympic medals—four gold and one bronze medal— and a world record in the 200m backstroke. She netted another spot in the record books when she added six gold medals at the FINA (Fédération Internationale de Natation) World Championship in Barcelona, Spain in 2013—winning more gold medals than any other female swimmer. Missy continued to rack up the medals and awards and now finds herself approaching what could be a repeat or better performance at the 2016 Olympics in Rio.

For many athletes there is a bonus to coming in first, second, or third place in a competition. Often there is a financial benefit awarded to them. These winnings, along with sponsorships and endorsements (think about the athletes we see advertising products) often make athletes very, very rich.

Accepting award money, or making money from advertising products or endorsing products has another affect—it makes an amateur athlete a professional athlete because they are being paid to play. As an elite athlete who passed on winnings from swimming events and what many guess to be millions of dollars in sponsorships and endorsements, Missy shows the value she places on being a normal teenager while being an exceptional athlete. Early on she decided against taking money for sponsorships from advertisers so that she could remain eligible to swim in college.

"Missy's special because she's unafraid to be herself, even when there's pressure to maybe be someone she's not," says her mother D.A. For Missy, being herself meant doing what many high school seniors dream of— going to college.

But first she would have to finish high school, not an easy task when swimming competitions have you travelling all over the country and the world. But for Missy Franklin, education was her first priority and it showed with a high school grade point average above a 4.0. Yet, while much of America—and the world—watched and cheered Missy on, there would still be those who would think less of her for what she would accomplish. Those with jealous hearts, who craved to have their own daughters share some of the limelight with Missy. Still, she kept her faith and she continued to pursue her swimming career and maintain her life in high school, using the talent and skill God gave her.

So, with the temptation to take the money and run, with the pressure from those who thought she shouldn't even compete at a high school level, weighing on her, Missy pressed on toward her dream to be an Olympian. For years, many have looked to four-time Olympian Michael Phelps as the reigning king of the Olympic waters. But now he has the reigning *queen* of Olympic waters drafting off him. In a 2011 interview with Jimmy Fallon, Phelps predicted what we already knew about Missy Franklin: "She is going to be someone to watch out for."

Missy Franklin Fast Facts

Hometown: Centennial, Colorado
Birthdate: May 10, 1995
High School: Regis Jesuit
College: University of California at Berkley
Parents: Dick and D.A. Franklin
Pet: Ruger, an Alaskan Malamute
First Swim Club: Heritage Green Gators
Hobbies: Reading, dancing, being with friends, baking
Olympics: 2012 in London
Olympic Medals: Five (4 gold, 1 bronze)

World Champs: Eleven (9 gold, 1 silver, 1 bronze)
International Medals: 38
USA Swimming National Team: 2014–2015
World Record: 200m backstroke (2.04.06)
American Record: 100m backstroke (58.33); 200y free-
    style (1:39:10)
Club: California Aquatics (CAL-CA)
Olympic and College Coach: Teri McKeever
Favorite CD: Taylor Swift 1984
Routine: Has her nails done with her mother before every
    competition
Must have: Travels with her teddy bear
Source: USA Swimming

Chapter 2

Missy Falls for the Water

Melissa Jeanette Franklin was born on May 10, 1995 and is the only child of D.A. and Dick Franklin. Missy has the distinction of having dual-citizenship—sharing citizenship with two countries—the U.S. and Canada. Missy was born in Pasadena, California but her parents are Canadian. Her mother is from Halifax, Nova Scotia, and her father is from St. Catharine's, Ontario.

Missy may get some of her athleticism from her father, Dick, who was an All-Canadian football player, playing for Saint Mary's University in Halifax, Nova Scotia. Dick took his football prowess one step further when he played as an offensive lineman for the Toronto Argonauts in the Canadian Football League. A football injury would send Dick back to college—Dalhousie University—for his MBA. God has a way of putting us where we need to be. D.A. was a medical student at the same university and the two met. Eventually Dick would have a career in business that would lead him to the US.

Both Dick and D.A. came from tough backgrounds. Dick had a demanding father who expected him to succeed in sports. When he did, Dick never received praise that should have come from his parents. D.A was a child of divorce, never seeing her mother after the age of six. During her early teens, she would nearly become a mother to her sister, helping to take care of her like a mother would. But somehow D.A. and her sister survived to adulthood. Dick moved up in the business world and D.A. and her sister both became doctors. D.A. eventually worked with the disabled while Dick began work at an environmental agency.

But besides professional success, Dick and D.A. had one more dream to fulfill—to have a child. It was no surprise that they viewed Missy as their miracle baby when she was born. As much older and wiser parents, Dick and D.A. turned out to be perfectly suited for raising a future Olympian, giving her all the love and support she needed. "When we finally had Missy, it was like, 'Ok, we're going to enjoy this.' We already had the BMW and the Porsches and the house. Now we could sit down in a rocking chair and bring this kid up," said Dick to *5280.com* of having Missy after both he and D.A had found considerable success in their respective careers.

Of course, Dick and D.A. had no way of knowing that Missy would be a future Olympian. But they did point her in the right direction from a very early age. D.A. had a fear of the water, but she didn't want her young daughter to have the same fear. When she was just six months old, D.A. like many new moms, enrolled the two of them in a Mom and Me swimming class. If it is possible for a baby to smile at six months—while under water—then Missy did just that. And if that wasn't enough to convince her parents that she belonged in the water, Missy set out to make it crystal clear.

This little girl loved water. When she was just four years old she was ready to join her first swim team. There was just one problem. She wasn't old enough. She had to wait until she was five. When she found out, she had something to say about it.

"Well, that's not fair," recalled Missy in an article in the NCAA *Champion* magazine. "I can swim better than any of them."

At five years old, Missy began swimming competitively, joining the Heritage Green Gators swim club in her neighborhood. She set her first record—a league record for girls six and under in the 25m backstroke. It seems fitting that she should win her first individual Olympic gold medal swimming the 100m backstroke.

At seven, she joined the Colorado Stars swim club and began working with Todd Schmitz. The young coach had previously worked in business but left to pursue his passion—swimming. His first day on the job was also Missy's first day with the swim club. Looking back on that time, Schmitz said Missy was a good swimmer who liked "racing superfast." But there was something missing. "She hadn't realized that she needed to translate that motivation into practicing," said Schmitz in the article. And by the time Missy was nine she won most of her races for the Colorado Stars.

Missy did what she needed to do, and by the time she was eleven, she was able to swim with older, more experienced swimmers, even replacing some of them in events. This didn't go over well with some of the swimmers, who were less than kind to Missy. D.A. told *5820.com* about that heartbreaking experience. Some teammates chose to ignore Missy at the end of a 400m relay. Like any mother who hurts when she sees her child being hurt, D.A. wanted to take care of it. Instead, Missy took care of it herself—by swimming in an event against the same girls and winning in spectacular fashion.

At an early age, Missy learned that it was better to show and not tell. She didn't need to engage in the meanness shown to her. She had to do only one thing. Swim. And she did that faster than others. "She had to prove herself," said D.A. in the same article. "She didn't have any problems after that."

Whether those girls chose to be Missy's friends or not didn't matter when it came to her swimming fast and winning. Sometimes the best way to silence an enemy is by getting in there and doing your best. This is what Missy Franklin showed them.

Missy tried other sports throughout her childhood. Basketball (you might think she had the height for that), volleyball (again a height advantage), soccer, ice skating, dancing, and gymnastics were some of the sports she tackled. She eliminated various sports interests one by one.

In an interview with *USA Swimming*, Missy described how she eliminated ice skating—or, to be more truthful, how it was eliminated for her. When she was young, her mother took her ice skating. D.A. went out on the ice, fell, and hit her head. That was the end of that. "She turned around and said, 'Okay, that's it—no more ice skating," recounted Missy.

Missy's parents exposed her to lots of sports to choose from, but eventually they had her focus on soccer, basketball, and swimming. Missy knew her parents wanted to give her several options to choose from. "My parents put in [sic] everything out there, and I learned something from each sport, and developed in a way I would not of [sic] had I not tried it," said Missy in the article. Missy even played on a volleyball team when she was in the seventh grade. The team was started by one of the parents of her club swim team. That volleyball team went on to win a state championship their very first year.

Missy also played volleyball in eighth grade at her school, even though she admits that she wasn't as coordinated playing volleyball as she was while swimming. But swimming would be king, and after eighth grade, all focus went to swimming.

By the age of twelve, Missy was gaining traction in the swim world. In 2008, at the age of thirteen, she qualified to swim in three events at the Olympic Trials for the Beijing Olympics, held in Omaha, Nebraska, giving her Colorado Stars swim team their first Olympic Trial qualifier.

No matter how fast or how good you are, all members of the US Olympic swim team must come through the Olympic trials and you need to place at least second to advance to the Olympics. Missy was declared a "Prodigy in the Swimming Pool" in a *DenverPost.com* article. According to the article, Missy was the second youngest swimmer to qualify. At thirteen years old, she was already standing 5'11" tall, ready to compete against some of the best female swimmers in the country. The Olympic Trials was the place where the stars came out to shine—Natalie Coughlin, Amanda Beard, Michael Phelps, Ryan Lochte, and Cullin Jones—all greats looking for their own spots on the Olympic team. Yet Missy was still Missy. Still thirteen. And still living at home in her purple bedroom. In the fall she would be going into the eighth grade at Powell Middle School.

Competing on a national stage for a chance to go to the Beijing Olympics might seem nerve-wracking for some but not for Missy Franklin. Looking at the upcoming event, Missy said, "There's no pressure." She was working toward a trip to the Beijing Olympics that would be held that August. Missy was still a middle school student. To even qualify for the Olympic Trials, Missy had to make qualifying times at other sanctioned meets. The tall but young competitor qualified to swim the 50m and the 100m freestyles, and the 200m individual medley. This was not only a first step but a feat for her to be proud of.

In spite of her efforts, Missy didn't make the team; but it was a great start for the young swimmer. She placed thirty-seventh in the 100m freestyle. Thirty-seventh was the highest mark she attained. And while that seems like a low placing in the overall competition, it helped guide her to her next major target—the trials for the London 2012 Olympics. Missy had four more years to get ready for the next Olympics. She would continue her quest by entering more and more contests, getting in the training and the wins she would need to compete on the next level. At one point, Missy's mother reminded her of her dual citizenship and the fact that she could compete for the Canadian team in the Olympics rather than the United States. Even knowing that the road to being a Canadian Olympian was not as hard as it was to be an American Olympian, Missy didn't want that.

"I don't think I could do that, I'm just so connected with the USA," said Missy in a *New York Times* article looking back at that time in her life. "When you walk out and you hear people chanting "USA" it's one of the best feelings in the world."

Missy loved being an American and the thought of representing the USA. She had chosen a hard road and this wouldn't be the last difficult decision she would make in her young swimming career.

Chapter 3

110 Percent

Sometimes it takes the movement of a car on the road, and some distance between where you are going and where you've been, to give perspective and time to process things. This is what happened to Missy Franklin. After swimming in three events in the Olympic trials in Omaha, Nebraska in 2008, Missy had a ride home with her parents that didn't include a fistful of medals. It didn't include a trip to Beijing. It didn't include the opportunity to represent the United States at the summer Olympics that year. But what it did include was the will to get to the next Olympic trials and the next Olympics.

"That was when it sort of hit me, that if I put 110 percent effort into every practice for the next four years, that I could have a shot at making the team in 2012," said Missy in an interview with the *Washington Post* in 2012. It was this type of focus that would occasionally put the young swimmer at odds with her friends who were not living in the world of competitive swimming. Being a swimmer aiming for Olympic competition requires a different mindset than most young people have.

"It was kind of hard for my friends to understand why I could never hang out and why I could never go to sleepovers and all this stuff," Franklin said in the *Daily Californian*. "That was kind of the time that I realized balancing this was going to be hard." Sleepovers are kind of hard to do when you are getting up and leaving for 5 a.m. swim sessions.

Missy was already doing more than many other swimmers her age, but she realized that she would have to take it up a notch if she wanted to make the 2012 Olympic team. She would continue to do what she did best—swim. Her next challenge would be doing it while trying to be a normal teenager swimming for her club—The Colorado Stars, for her country on the USA Swimming National Team, and for the Raiders—her future high school team. Needless to say, Regis Jesuit High School in Aurora, Colorado, welcomed swimming sensation Missy Franklin with open arms to their swim team.

For many of us, faith has always been a part of our life, but for Missy Franklin, faith in God wasn't something that she was born into. Missy's parents, D.A. and Dick, didn't profess any particular faith, and religion wasn't a priority for them while raising their daughter. The Franklins never had a church home, and when they did go to church, Missy felt uncomfortable and out of sorts, not knowing how to act or what to expect. But that all changed when she decided to attend Regis Jesuit Catholic High School.

In an interview with *beliefnet.com*, Missy talked about a visit to what would become her new high school: "As I walked in the main door, I felt at peace and I knew I belonged there. From that first moment, I knew God was with me."

Missy and her club swim coach were racking up awards and recognition for the work they were doing. Colorado Stars coach Todd Schmitz won the Age Group Coach of the Year award from the American Swim Coaches Association (ASCA) in September. He followed that up with the same award from Colorado Swimming. October was good to Missy as well, with her winning the Swimmer of the Year award from Colorado Swimming.

Missy and Schmitz actually had back-to-back good years. Schmitz would again win the Age Group Coach of the Year award from the American Swim Coaches Association. And he would take the Senior Coach of the Year award from Colorado Swimming. Missy would repeat as the Swimmer of the Year from Colorado Swimming.

Little did the private Catholic high school know what was in store. Immediately, Missy started making waves—good ones—in their swim program. She showed up with multiple national records behind her and nothing but a promising future in front of her. Even as a freshman, she was the talk of the town, and that included with the coaches of her competition. It's hard not to notice who your team will be going up against. "That will be the individual that has everybody going, 'Oh, boy,'" said Rampart Rams (Colorado Springs, Colorado) swim coach Pat Burch about Missy in an interview with the *Denver Post*.

Missy's first major high school swim meet went on without her—she was across the Big Pond in England swimming for the United States in the Duel in the Pool. USA Swimming National Team Director Frank Busch calls the Duel in the Pool competition, ". . . one of the most exciting events on the international swimming calendar." This USA versus Europe swim meet features the best of American and European swimmers in a short-course competition. The first Duel in the Pool was in 2003 and has been held every two years since then. The Indiana University Natatorium hosted the first Duel in the Pool.

The freshman in high school raced 100m freestyle relay leg at 52.78 seconds, giving Missy the seventh fastest time in the world for that leg of the race. She gave her same best when she competed at her high school swim meets.

Missy, 15, jokes with friends during her practice with the Regis Jesuit High School swim team in 2011.

Missy's Regis Raiders team was swimming in the 5A division. She was being compared to another strong swimmer in the region, Bonnie Brandon, a sophomore at the time with four state titles who had broken records in each of her events. The season was setting itself up nicely for some friendly competition between the two top-ten swim teams—Brandon's Cherry Creek and Franklin's Regis Jesuit. At the time of the article, Missy had captured a second place finish in the 200m individual medley at the FINA World Cup championships in Stockholm. *The Denver Post* had Missy Franklin listed under "swimmers to watch."

The world was already watching Missy. She had landed on the cover of *Swimming World Magazine*. She held 10 national swimming records. She was training up to five hours a day—clearly keeping her promise to herself to give 110 percent in practices. But she was still having fun, according to her Colorado Stars swim coach, Todd Schmitz. Schmitz worked to make sure that Missy and her teammates remained "typical" teenagers.

"They'll still want to get out early on a Friday night and go to a football game, and there's value to that too," said Schmitz in an interview with the *Denver Post*. "As a coach, you have to know when do you push and when do you not."

Practice for Missy wasn't all about swimming. Her training included dryland workouts such as running, biking, and even Pilates. According to Missy's instructor, Ann Daxberger, Pilates not only helps to strengthen the extensors, rotators, and deep abdominal muscles to improve alignment, it also helps athletes concentrate on breath control. The Pilates works to "counter the

Cyrus McCrimmon/The Denver Post via Getty Images

Practice for Missy isn't all about swimming. Her training includes dryland workouts such as running, biking, and even Pilates.

round-shouldered" profile of many swimmers. These exercises, even though they were out of the water, were part of Missy's 110 percent as well.

Missy continued to wow fans and other swimmers alike as she kept her positive attitude about what she was doing. She was also traveling the world with some of the greatest swimmers on earth. It was nothing for her to be with swimmers like Michael Phelps. Yet she wasn't an awestruck teenager while swimming with these greats. They were her peers in the water. And she remained just "Missy the teenager" when at school and around her friends.

"I surprise myself every time I get in the water," said Missy in another *Denver Post* article. "I honestly have no idea what's going to happen." This attitude showed her sincerity about the great job she was doing. Somehow she never came off as self-important, and she carried herself with the attitude of a developing champion— and still does.

"She doesn't create resentment from people, she creates that enthusiasm and excitement," said Nick Frasersmith, her Regis coach. In the same article he noted that it was tough for anyone to resent her. He felt it was Missy's attitude that kept the competition all about swimming, not about her.

And competition would always be waiting for her, whether on the international stage or a high school swim meet. This was the case in February 2010 when Franklin went up against serious competition at the 5A swimming and diving championships at Edora Pool and Ice Center in Fort Collins, Colorado. Rampart Rams swimmer Jenna Gregoire was the record holder in the 100y freestyle. Gregoire also competed in the 50y freestyle. But there was one ripple in the pool that could possibly keep Gregoire from achieving her goal of winning this particular year. Missy Franklin.

Missy was such a threat that the Rampart's coach, Pat Burch, told Gregoire she could swim a different event so she wouldn't have to go up against Missy Franklin. But Gregoire let Burch know she wanted to go head-to-head with the swimmer who was holding her own at international levels.

As it turned out, Franklin dominated at the meet, placing a time of 22.70 in the 50y freestyle and 53.43 in the 100y backstroke, both Colorado state records. Still, school rival Cherry Creek won the state title for the sixth consecutive time. But this was just her freshman year. Missy loved the "team aspect" of high school sports.

She loved bonding with her teammates. There was still time for the team to come together to win a state title.

On an individual level, Missy was given the distinction of being All-Colorado in girls swimming for the 50y freestyle and the 100y backstroke. She was also named Swimmer of the Year for the 2010 season. It was a repeat in Class 5A—50y freestyle, the 100y backstroke, and Swimmer of the Year.

Missy was having a banner year as a freshman at Regis. In a fast-facts article for the *Denver Post,* Missy credited her high school with helping her grow academically (and her parents as well). Often, the school would allow Missy to make up tests—in the principal's office on a Saturday if necessary—so that she could maintain her Team USA swim schedule. It was what she needed if she was going to keep up with being both a normal high school student and an international swimming sensation.

Missy at 14, Regis Jesuit,
The Denver Post

Favorite subject: chemistry
Favorite athlete: Olympic swimmer Natalie Coughlin
Music: Everything except heavy metal "scream music"
Thumbs Up: Being on a team and bonding
Thumbs Down: 5:00 a.m. swim practices

Chapter 4

Sophomore Sensation

Missy entered her sophomore year of high school and it didn't look like she had any intention of slowing down. If anything, she was getting faster. An incident the summer before reset the stage for who she was and who she would become as a swimmer. In an article from the *New York Times*, Missy's parents and swim coach spoke about their strategy to get Missy to where she ultimately wanted to be—the Olympic Games in London, England.

In a move that bothered the United States national team coach, Mark Schubert, Missy was not entered into the world championship trials in Rome. This would have been a competition very much like what Missy might face in the Olympic Games. Instead, she was entered in the junior national championship. Missy would be going up against swimmers closer to her own age.

This did not go over well with Schubert, but Missy's parents, Dick and D.A., along with her Colorado Stars coach, Todd Schmitz, stood firm on their decision. "The question at the end of the day was, 'Is that going to help us on our journey to the 2012 Olympics?' We thought she would benefit more from the experience of racing in a lot of events," said Schmitz in the same *New York Times* article.

Once again Missy was stellar in competition, scoring the sixth-fastest time by an American woman in the 100m freestyle. If she had competed in Rome, her time of 54.03 seconds would have had her sharing the podium as a second place finisher with another swimmer. Missy won the high-point trophy at the junior national competition. "I think it was a really good idea to swim at junior nationals. We just didn't want to skip any steps," said Missy in the *Times* article.

Following a strategy was what Missy was all about. She had a mission and she stayed true to herself and found success. But sometimes following a plan put her at odds with her school schedule. Lucky for Missy, Regis Jesuit was willing to work with her.

Again, Missy would miss classes to compete for the United States at the Pan Pacific Championships in Irvine, California, an event that included swimmers from non-European countries. Missy would go on to a fourth place finish in the 100m backstroke at that event.

Missy continued to put in 5 a.m. practices, leaving the house while it was still dark outside. Her dedication to making it to the Olympics in 2012 was stronger than the average teenager's desire to stay in bed for a few more zzz's. And that dedication was paying off on the podium as she continued to collect swimming hardware—a nickname for medals.

In November 2010, she picked up another win in the women's 200y freestyle at the USA Swimming Grand

Prix in Minneapolis. She also took the 400y individual medley. Her career best time came in the 200y individual medley. Gold was waiting for her in the 200y backstroke and the 100y freestyle. A silver in the 400y freestyle relay and bronze in the 400y medley and the 800y medley freestyle relays rounded out the three-day event. In total, Missy swam away with seven medals from seven events at the Grand Prix. Again, she was awarded for her hard work with The Denver Post Youth Excellence in Sports award for the month of November.

Missy swam with the Colorado Stars at the US Short Course National Championship in Columbus, Ohio where she finished third in the 200y individual medley. She had a fourth-place finish in the 50y freestyle. Another notable award was waiting for her. Missy's competitions didn't go unnoticed by USA Swimming, and it was no surprise that she would take home a Golden Goggle Award for Breakout Performer of the Year in 2010.

Missy wasn't just swimming in the fast lane. She was all over the US and the world in swimming competitions, while friends her age were hanging out in the mall, enjoying movies and sleepovers. Skype kept her in touch with friends, but that was as good as it got. "These are the sacrifices you have to make to be the best in your sport. I would do everything the same if I had to do it again," said Missy in a *Denver Post* article. At the same time, Missy was sharing newspaper headlines with Olympic swimmers who were becoming her friends. "It means the world to me when they tell me I have done well," said Missy.

The London Olympic trials were about a year and a half away, but USA Swimming coach Teri McKeever was already speculating on Missy's participation in the Olympics. McKeever saw Missy's potential to be in London as a "great possibility," according to the *Post*. But first things first. Missy would have to take on the World Championships in Dubai, United Arab Emirates in December, 2010.

Again Missy would be traveling across the world to compete with other stellar athletes for the USA. She started out with a fourth place finish in the 100m backstroke at the World Championships, but picked up a silver medal in the 200m backstroke. She also placed seventh in the 100m individual medley. This was still a great showing for someone as young as Missy.

Back in the states, Missy swam at the Austin Grand Prix. She came out on top with 28 points, winning five events. Finishing in the number one spot put Missy in line to win the overall Grand Prix series prize money. But even if she did come out of the seven-meet series on top, she wouldn't take the money. In addition to her goal to swim at the London Olympics, Missy wanted to swim in college. And that meant avoiding anything that would make her ineligible. Prize money, sponsorships— anything that could keep her from her college goal—was left on the table.

Missy was constantly in the pool, making waves and draping more hardware around her neck. She had already helped her high school team end the reign of local rival Cherry Creek by winning their state meet her sophomore year. She was making the covers of magazines and winning titles. Michael Phelps said, "She can get out and swim with anybody, and isn't at all fazed by it," in an *ESPN.com* article.

By the summer before her junior year, everyone who was anyone in the swimming world had taken notice of Missy. She won five medals at the World Championships in Shanghai, including three gold. She won two more titles at the US National Championships in California. That was just two days after the World Championships. While this much attention might leave some people star-struck with themselves, Missy remained as humble as ever, even giving away one of her gold medals from nationals to a young basket girl, whose job was to collect swimmers' clothes on the deck. The little girl, Olivia, and her father approached Missy the next day and thanked her. "It means more to them," Missy told the *Denver Post*.

Australia Belinda Hocking (silver), Missy (gold), and The Netherlands Sharon Van Rouwendaal (bronze) victorious on medal stand after winning the Women's 200m Backstroke Final at the 2011 FINA World Championships in China.

Missy was well on the path to the 2012 Olympics when she set a short course world record in the 200m backstroke at the World Cup meet in Berlin, Germany. And Missy was closing out 2011 with a Golden Goggle Award for Best Female Athlete. All of this success didn't take its toll on Missy's studies however. Even while traveling to Atlanta for the Duel in the Pool, between the US and Europe, Missy was making flashcards for final exams. "I like being a student. I like going to school every day," she told *ESPN.com*.

Her ability to be in both the academic and the competitive swimming worlds on a successful level may have kept her grounded as she continued to explode in the swim world. Even with the money that companies were eager to throw at her, Missy stayed focused on the real prize, which for her was remaining an amateur, competing in the Olympics, and going to college rather than getting all the money and sponsorships yet.

Finding Faith

During her junior year in high school Missy attended a spiritual retreat through Regis Jesuit. The retreat, *Kairos*, was shrouded in secrecy. The word *kairos* is Greek and means "a time when conditions are right for the accomplishment of a crucial action," according to the Merriam-Webster online dictionary. For four days the students attended the retreat, focused on "Who am I and where am I going?" according to Regis Athletic Director John Koslosky. Students also volunteered in a community service project. According to an article in *The Guardian*, Missy's volunteer assignment included working with low-income children whose parents couldn't afford daytime childcare. The tall teenager worked with kids ages three to five. "It was probably one of the two or three best weeks of my life, just to be there, help them and play with them," said Missy.

Missy was making a statement about who she was. Missy had been at the school for three years, a time in which she had seen her faith steadily grow. Attending a *Kairos* retreat with her Regis Jesuit sisters as well as the service trip changed her life forever, according to Missy. Like many average teenage girls, Missy learned what it meant to have a relationship with God. Without giving any details about the event, Missy said it was one of the most incredible experiences she had ever had. "I now really work on keeping my faith strong," she said of the event.

Missy's faith was growing and guiding her. "God is always there for me. I talk with Him before, during, and after practice and competitions. I pray to Him for guidance," says Missy. "I thank Him for this talent He has given me and promise to be a positive role model for young athletes in all sports," said Missy in an interview with *Belief.net.*

The busy swimmer not only participated in the *Kairos* retreat. She was also preparing for the Olympics. Missy made both events work by driving from the Olympic Training Center in Colorado to the retreat held south of Denver. Her commitment to both was just part of her dual life as a student with a passion for God and a swimmer with a passion for winning. Whether she knew it or not, Missy had become a role model for more than young athletes. She had become someone the world could look up to. And she did it with a humble heart and a busy life.

Chapter 5

The Olympic Trials—
Keeping Promises

This was it. Everything that Missy had done the past four years—the early morning practices, the competitions around the country and all over the world—had led up to this near-Olympic moment. Four years earlier, she had been one of the youngest swimmers at the Olympic Trials in Omaha, Nebraska. She had been just 13 years old, not even in high school. Even though she had been churning out some of the best swim times leading to the trials, she hadn't made the cut to compete in the 2008 Olympics in Beijing. But she had made a promise to herself. This would be Missy's chance to face her fate—what she had been working so hard for, with God's help and strength.

In an article on *ThePostGame.com*, Missy reflected on where she had been four years before. "I remember sitting down there in the ready room during prelims before I swam, going, 'In four years I want to be sitting right here, and I want to have a good shot at making the team,'" said Missy. "And that's what's really motivated me for the past four years, is just that feeling I had sitting there, just knowing that in four years, I was going to come back and I was going to be ready."

The world had been watching her build up to the trials, and in a prophetic moment at Dove Valley, the NFL Bronco's practice facility, Missy was given a football signed by the Denver Broncos teammates and Denver Broncos General Manager, Executive Vice President of Football Operations, and football legend John Elway. The message on the ball left little room for doubt about where they felt Missy's future was headed: "Great things are going to happen. Good luck."

Great things had been happening for the teenaged swimmer who consistently worked on improving herself. She was doing what she felt she needed to do to compete on the world stage—the ultimate stage—the Olympics. She was giving 110 percent—maybe more. Her mind was so focused on the task at hand, that right before the trials, she had a dream she had missed an event. While a dream like that proves Missy Franklin is indeed human, she had nothing to worry about. She would be ready. She would be herself—lighthearted, always smiling, dancing if the music was right, and then stepping up to the blocks, and just like that—flipping the switch.

The switch was on when Missy took to her first race at the Olympic Trials in Omaha. The fact was this: they would only take the top two finishers to the London Olympics. It wouldn't matter how well she had done anywhere else, how many medals she had collected, or what

Missy Franklin starts in the women's 100m backstroke preliminaries at the U.S. Olympic swimming trials, Tuesday, June 26, 2012, in Omaha, NE.

AP Images/David J. Phillip

records she had already broken. It came down to her performance in the finals. The top two would go. Period.

The first race Missy swam in was the preliminary heat of the women's 100m backstroke. Her time was 59.54 seconds, the fifth-fastest time in the world, at that time. Missy was in the number two spot, seeded behind Natalie Coughlin for the semifinal that evening. The next evening, Missy would not only steal the lead from the swimmer she greatly respected, she would set an American record.

Missy had just finished qualifying for Thursday night's 200m freestyle. Even though she came in fifth, it didn't seem to bother her as she prepared to swim her next race, with only 18 minutes between the races. Missy swam next to Rachel Bootsma. Natalie Coughlin, who had set a faster time than Missy in the prelims, was two lanes over. Missy's Olympic moment, four years in the making, was now here, just 100m away. It would just take reaching the touchpad first.

How long does it take to make an Olympian? A lifetime of practicing? Four years after a failed attempt? 58.85 seconds. That was all it took for Missy to set a record. When she hit the touchpad first, Missy's flight for London was booked. This win meant that she was on her way to the 2012 Olympic Games!

Rachel Bootsma came in second, and Natalie Coughlin, who had been the reigning gold medalist in that event, came in third. "It's time for Missy," commented Coughlin after Missy's record-setting race. Both swimmers were gracious, with Missy complimenting the woman she had always looked up to. "I have learned so much from her, and I plan to learn so much from her. She still has other chances to make the team, and I am absolutely praying for her that she does because I want to learn more from her, and I would love to be on another team with her," said Missy in an *ESPN.com* interview. Even in the pure excitement of her victory, Missy was quick to offer up a prayer and well-wishes for her fellow swimming teammate.

Reflecting on the victory that made her an Olympian, Missy said that the short time between the races may have helped her. She didn't have time to worry about how she had previously placed in her race, or how she would do in the next one. "I love doing back-to-backs, and I didn't have time to get nervous for the 100 back, so it worked out perfectly," said Missy.

Coughlin praised Missy for pulling off a win, particularly so close after another race. She herself had raced "doubles" while in college, and during short-course events. She was impressed with how Missy handled doubles in a long-course, under so much pressure.

Todd Schmitz watched Missy go into the two races confident that she would be able to pull it off. "I'd be the first one to tell you that if she didn't [qualify] in that 100 back, I'd put my credential (identification tag that gave him access to the event) down and walk off the pool deck," said Schmitz in the *ESPN* article. "I look like a genius now, but I could have gone the other way."

For Missy, the swim was about doing what she said she would do four years previous. "I have dreamed of this moment, but I never thought it would come true at 17 years old," said Franklin to *ESPN.com*. "Dreams do come true."

Dick and D.A. Franklin shared in the joy of having a daughter make the US Olympic team. All of those early morning drives to swim practice, all of the traveling to swim meets, all they had done for Missy to see her dream through, had just paid off. "We were totally shocked. We were ecstatic when she won her first qualifying event," said Dick in the *Daily Californian*. Missy's parents had never been the type to be pushy or think less of their daughter if she didn't succeed. They just wanted her to be happy and have fun. Dick continued, "We had an Olympian, and if it had ended there, it would have been enough."

While Missy had secured a spot on the Olympic team, there were still other races at the trials. Missy Franklin was not one to sit back and take it easy. But her parents still had one goal in mind for her—to have fun and still be a normal kid. That had been Missy's approach for most of her life. It was one reason she decided not to take any money for winning or sponsorships. She knew that the moment she became a professional swimmer, swimming would be work. There would be expectations set by others, not by herself or her coach who knew her well. And if you didn't deliver, you wouldn't get the money. But for now, swimming was fun. Being a teenager was fun. Being Missy Franklin, an Olympian, was fun.

The next event Missy qualified for was the 200m freestyle. She finished second in that event, again good enough to go to the Olympics. She got another second place finish in the 100 freestyle. Her 200m backstroke time of 2:06.12 was the fastest backstroke in the world that year. Twelve events and six days later, Missy was eligible to swim in seven events in London—her four individual events, and three relays. She was the first American woman to qualify for seven events in one Olympic Game, according to an article in the *Guardian*, a fact that surprised Missy who said she was both overwhelmed and excited at the same time.

Missy had gone from not making the team four years prior to qualifying for seven events in 2012. She had not let the setback in 2008 remain a setback. She had used it to propel herself further and faster.

Her coach called her a true gamer that just kept rolling along. Schmitz said that some people would be satisfied with their first spot. But not Missy. According to Schmitz, she was relieved, but not completely satisfied. For Missy, the next step would be the actual Olympics Games. Satisfaction wasn't too far away.

Now that the Olympic swim team was set and Missy had found her place on it for seven events, she had other things to do. Like Olympic Training camp. "It has been so much fun just being able to lie in bed at night and realize that I am at an Olympic training camp," said Missy in an AP article. "It's just the coolest thing ever and getting to know my teammates so much more. The training camp in Knoxville, Tennessee was just a precursor to a training camp in France."

The city of Knoxville welcomed the Olympians, wishing them luck and congratulating them. Missy was impressed that the whole town was behind them. She would soon find out that the whole country was behind the team too.

Chapter 6

Olympic Coach Teri McKeever

What does it take to coach an Olympian? Why an Olympic coach, and not just any coach? These were the best of the best athletes, going to the world's greatest competition. And these athletes need the best coaches in the world.

The obvious challenge for the coach, the athlete, and the whole Olympic team, is to bring home the hardware. This is what newly-minted Olympian Missy Franklin found out. She was now part of the United States Olympic women's swim team and it would be led by the first-ever United States female head coach.

The coach wasn't magically granted this position, she had more than earned it. Coach Teri McKeever had already made appearances at the Olympics as an assistant coach in 2004 and in 2008, and she had been the head coach of the University of California at Berkeley's swim team for over 20 years. So this was not her first rodeo.

But what does USA Swimming look for in an Olympic coach? An Olympic caliber coach must be able to lead the team to win national championships on the Olympic level and deliver international medalists year after year, according to Frank Busch, the national team director for USA Swimming. Teri McKeever was already proving she could deliver. She had mentored a number of Olympians, including Natalie Coughlin. In an *SFGate.com* article Coughlin said, "She's definitely paid her dues. I can't think of another female who deserves the title [more in US swimming.]" Coughlin should know. She has eleven Olympic medals since training under McKeever.

Of course, like many successful people, McKeever made some sacrifices along the way, to get where she was. Working to get to the level of an Olympic coach meant doing more and more professionally, with little time for herself. She married for the first time at age 45. And she didn't have children of her own. It takes extra commitment says McKeever.

There is admittedly some regret on her part, but she wouldn't change anything now, says McKeever. She knew the kinds of sacrifices she would have to make to be a coach at this level. "I think coaching at the highest level is a lifestyle kind of job," said McKeever in the *SFGate* article. "It's hard for women to have the time." And McKeever knows firsthand about women making time for family and career.

Teri McKeever was born in 1962 to Judy and Mike McKeever. Mike was a football player for the University of Southern California (USC). Her mother had been a competitive swimmer. In 1965 Teri's father was in a car accident that left him in a coma for 22 months. He died in 1967. Teri had two siblings at the time. Her mother eventually remarried and had seven more children and Teri helped out with her younger siblings. But she learned to swim even with all the family responsibilities, using the family's 25y backyard pool. Her mother coached her. "For me, sports was the first place I felt good about myself," McKeever said in an interview in the New York Times.

McKeever pursued her swimming career in high school. Participating in swim meets gave her precious alone time with her mother. McKeever went on to be an All-American swimmer in college. She graduated with a degree in education and earned a spot as the women's assistant coach for the swim team at USC while earning a master's degree in athletic administration. She worked there until 1987 then took a position as the head swim coach at Fresno State. Five years later she moved to the University of California at Berkeley and has been there ever since. When it was announced that she would be the head coach for the women's Olympic team, Teri felt honored. But the moment that really had her on an emotional high was when she told her mother. It was a lifetime of hard work being recognized, and who better to share it with than the woman who had helped her get to where she was?

McKeever is known for her somewhat unconventional training methods. Swimmers don't just pound it out in the pool when they train with Teri; they are taking hip-hop classes and doing Pilates and other things that don't add up to yards and yards of swimming. Her unconventional ways have turned out other Olympians besides Missy Franklin. Natalie Coughlin netted 11 Olympic medals under McKeever and she helped Dana Vollmer pick up the pieces after an unsuccessful 2008 run for the Olympics. Even Olympian Anthony Ervin returned to Cal to train with the women's swim team under McKeever.

Ervin, who won a gold medal when he was just 18, returned to competition 12 years later. He recognized that McKeever was someone who could work with him, preparing him both physically and mentally. "And she brought back what it was like to swim for fun and enjoy myself," said Ervin in a *New York Times* article.

Vollmer, Ervin, and Coughlin all qualified for the 2012 Olympics. Ervin placed fifth in the 50m freestyle. Coughlin received a bronze medal in the 400m freestyle relay. Vollmer received three gold medals at the London Olympics—one in the 800m freestyle relay, one in the 400m medley relay (setting a world record), and one in the 100m butterfly (setting another world record). When Vollmer started swimming at Cal, she came with a pack of injuries. But with McKeever, she was ready to redeem herself from her 2008 failure to qualify for the Beijing Olympics. McKeever's coaching talent didn't stop at helping Olympic swimmers so they could compete again. She worked to make them successful in all their competitions.

And then there was Missy Franklin. She hadn't yet trained under McKeever. But from the time of the trials to the start of the Olympics there were just twenty-six days for the team to get it all together. Missy would find herself under the watchful instruction of Teri McKeever. Missy's speed had made her an Olympian at the trials in Omaha, Nebraska. McKeever would help to make her a winner in London.

Chapter 7

Ready, Set, Go

The second training camp in France wouldn't be all about land and water exercises and swimming. At their first training camp in Knoxville, Tennessee, the team and their coaches got a chance to get to know each other. The 49-member team would have the opportunity to gel—come together—before the upcoming Olympics. The Olympians would put in hard work to get into the best shape ever both physically and mentally before heading to their next training camp. A week later, they would be in Vichy, France.

This camp was described as "low-key" in a *Rueters.com* article. "This week has been about fixing all those little things that can make a big difference," said Olympic great Michael Phelps. Missy echoed her teammate's view of the camp.

"The whole environment has been fantastic and absolutely we'll go faster in London. We've been working really hard on the small things and now we're ready."

Assistant Olympic coach Todd Schmitz described the camp as more technical, while the camp in Tennessee was intended to increase volume. "It's been more a resting and preparation camp than a training camp," said Schmitz in the *Rueters.com* article.

In addition to the fine-tuning, there was fun to be had in Vichy. There, Missy, along with other Olympic swim team rookies would have to perform a skit for their more seasoned teammates. This was all part of what it would take for the team to come together to compete at the London Olympics which would begin on July 27, 2010. At the last Olympics, the rookies performed karaoke. This Olympic camp would include a little of Missy's favorite past-time—dancing. Initially, Missy seemed shy about dancing in front of everyone. But that all changed once she actually started dancing, said Natalie Coughlin. It's hard to believe that the smiling, dancing swimmer could be shy about performing before her teammates, particularly since she and others on the Olympic swim team put together their own little send off when they grooved to Carly Rae Jepsen's *Call Me Maybe*. Missy held her own singing and dancing down the aisle of their airplane.

The fun and camaraderie of training camps would give way to the beginning of the Olympics. Franklin would be representing the USA in seven swimming events. This was what she had trained her whole life for, what she knew she was meant to do since she was a very little girl drawing Olympic circles—even before she really knew what it meant to be an Olympian. With many swimming events and medals behind her, Missy was about to go to the one event that would forever define her as an Olympian. And she did not forget God.

In an interview with Chad Bonham for *beliefnet.com*, Bonham asked the Olympian what her expectations were for what God might be doing through the church at the Olympics. Missy's response spoke to her faith that God was and would be right there with her.

"Once every four years, athletes, families, friends, and fans come together from all over the world. I know God will be there and I hope many of the people there will also feel His presence," stated Missy in the interview. "He will offer us the opportunity to appreciate and love our similarities and differences. It will be up to each of us to take away as little or as much as we want from London."

All of her preparation, skill, ability, and her God-given made-for-swimming body helped Missy be ready to compete on the world stage of the Olympics. And her great attitude and faith in God allowed her to be a shining example to fans the world over. But tragedy would strike not far from her home. And her response would prove to the world the kind of person we already knew Missy to be.

While Missy was across the ocean at the pre-Olympic Games training camp in Vichy, France, preparing to compete for her country, a young man was in her hometown, in a movie theater where her friends might be, planning an unimaginable act of terrorism against the defenseless. Missy received a message from her mother letting her know of a tragedy that occurred just miles from her high school.

News media from all over the country reported on the small town of Aurora, Colorado, and this time it would not be to cover their Olympian, Missy Franklin.

The country and the world would be looking at another senseless shooting incident.

At midnight on July 20, 2012, just five days before the start of the 2012 London Olympics, a gas mask-wearing gunman entered a movie theater screening of *Batman, The Dark Knight Rises*. The gunman would later be identified as James Eagan Holmes, a 24-year-old doctoral candidate in the neuroscience program at the Anschutz Medical Campus in Aurora, Colorado. The same city where Missy attended high school.

Holmes had purchased a ticket to the movie on July 7th for the July 20th midnight showing at the Century Aurora 16 Multiplex Theater. He arrived early to the theater, sat in the front row, and a few minutes into the movie, Holmes left by the emergency exit, a door he had left propped open. He returned wearing protective gear covering his entire body, including a ballistic helmet (to protect himself from gunshots to the head). He was also wearing a gas mask, which protected him from the tear gas canisters he threw into the theater. It was then that he began shooting. A total of twelve people were killed and 58 were wounded.

Holmes turned himself into police outside the theater. It was later found that Holmes had made bombs and left them inside his apartment. He was charged with 142 counts including multiple counts of first-degree murder and attempted murder, as well as felony possession of explosive devices.

There is no doubt that Missy's parents wanted to be with their daughter during this tragedy. Her father reached out to coach McKeever. He knew that Missy would be worried about whether any of her friends had have been at the premiere. Teri McKeever talked about

Missy's response to the tragedy in an article in the *L.A. Times*. McKeever said she made her way to Missy's room. "I just knocked on the door and asked how she was doing," McKeever said. "We talked about when you grow up that you see more and more hard things. That's kind of what sucks sometimes about growing up."

Missy was immediately concerned about friends who had planned to go to the premiere, as well as for the other victims and their families. "I am both shocked and deeply saddened by the shooting that took place in Colorado. Aurora is my hometown, and my thoughts and prayers go out to all the friends and families affected by this senseless tragedy," said Missy, as reported in a *New York Times* article.

Like many kids her age, Missy took to social media and posted this on her official account on Twitter @ FranklinMissy: "Praying for everyone hurt and affected by the theater shooting in Aurora. I'm in total disbelief and shock. Things happen so quickly." Missy ended her tweet with "#pray." It is times like these when prayer is absolutely the best response.

Todd Schmitz, assistant Olympic Coach, along with many of Missy's USA teammates responded via Twitter to the tragedy. Schmitz posted on Twitter, "My thoughts are with everyone back in my home of Aurora, Colorado #theatershooting." Swimmers Ryan Lochte and Jessica Hardy also shared their thoughts with the world. Jessica quoted Helen Keller in her tweet when she said, "Faith is strength by which a shattered world shall emerge into the light."

While the world ached with sympathy over the tragic events in Aurora, Missy didn't limit her feelings to her social media posts. She took it one step further. She dedicated her wins to Colorado. "Right now, all of my races are dedicated back home to Colorado," said Missy in an *L.A. Times* article. "No matter how well I do, I'm going to give my best in every single race, and every single race, I'm going to have that Colorado incident on my mind," said Missy. "They're in my thoughts through this entire process."

We may never know why people commit horrible acts, but we do know that God is always with us, regardless of the events and outcomes. And we know that no matter how painful the event, we can't let it stop us, keep us from living our lives. That is not who God would have us be. Missy still had a mission. And God was still with her as she used her God-given talents for his glory.

Chapter 8

London 2012

Missy Franklin was ready for world competition—100 percent ready. But was the world ready for Missy Franklin? They had certainly heard of her. She had grown taller, faster, and wiser since her first run for the Olympics in 2008. She had collected medal after medal, award after award in the ensuing years. She even left the Olympic trials with an award—an Omega watch for Female Swimmer of the Meet. Now came the time she had been training for her whole life. It was the fulfillment of the promise she had made to herself four years before. And the world would be watching.

Athletes, representing countries from all around the world, were set to march in the 2012 London Olympic opening ceremonies. Except Missy Franklin. She would be sitting this part out. The grand opening ceremony would begin on July 27 at 9:00 p.m. and would go until just after midnight. That wouldn't give Missy enough time to rest for her first race the next morning. And with seven events in eight days, more than any other American woman had ever competed in at a single Olympics, Missy would have her work cut out for her. Again, she would make a sacrifice for the ultimate goal of getting an Olympic medal, this time by sitting out of the incredible opening ceremonies.

Franklin was relaxed and ready to swim the next day. "It feels like it did before World's last year, I feel so comfortable. I've never felt so ready to race before," said Franklin in a *Denver Post* article. And she was ready. Missy, along with Jessica Hardy, Lia Neal, and Allison Schmitt snagged her first Olympic medal—bronze— when the team came in 3rd in the 400m freestyle relay. Missy swam the first leg of the race, setting a personal best and age group record time of 53.52 for the first 100m. Missy's powerful swim put the Americans in the lead.

Franklin admitted to making necessary changes to the way she swam. Her changes made her faster than her times in Omaha during the trials. It also helped that Missy didn't swim in the prelims for the race—a decision that would help save her body for the other races she had that week.

Their team time was 3:34.24 behind the Netherlands who came in second with a time of 3:33.79, and Australia who won gold with a time of 3:33.15. The bronze medal would mean so much to Missy because it was her first. And she was just getting started.

"I have dreamed about this my whole life," said Franklin in a *Denver Post* article. "I honestly couldn't be happier."

Missy was taking in "every single moment"—a piece of advice she had been given. The Olympics were the pinnacle of her career and it would be a shame to miss out on any of it. "Some of the girls on the team said their first Olympics they were so focused on what they were doing they didn't have as much fun as they wanted to. Having them say that put everything in perspective," said Missy to the *Denver Post*. Having fun and being prepared were defining characteristics of Missy Franklin. Her ever-constant smile left no doubt about that. And the fact that she came in relaxed backed it all up. Now all she had to do was swim in six more events.

Not only did Missy swim in the final events, she would also swim in some prelims—the events that would get her to those semis and the finals. In one day, she would swim in the preliminary heat of the women's 200m freestyle, setting the third fastest time, placing her in the semifinals that evening. She would follow that up just 14 minutes later with the 100m backstroke final. As we know, swimming so many races so close together wasn't a new challenge for Missy. She had been in enough world-class events with back-to-back races that she was more than ready. Keeping to her true nature, Missy told *ESPN.com*, "It's going to be fun. I need to keep my energy up as much as possible and do the best I can do and just be proud of myself. It's going to be tough for sure."

For Missy Franklin, tough didn't translate to impossible.

Olympics 2016

Location: Rio De Janiero, Brazil
Date: August 5-21, 2016; Paralympic Games will be held
 September 7-18, 2016

Right before the race, while all of the swimmers stood on the deck in front of their lanes, Missy did a little shoulder-arm-loosen-up wiggle. She took a visible deep breath and let it out. And then she smiled her signature smile. There was nothing left to do but swim.

On the turn at the split, Missy was in third place behind Australia's Emily Seebohm and Russia's Anastasia Zueva. Missy poured it on during the last 50m reaching the touchpad just .35 seconds ahead of Seebohm. It was enough for gold.

Missy went on to express how that moment on the podium, after the race, felt to her: ". . . seeing that flag being raised was so incredibly unbelievable. I could have never dreamed it would feel like that." This was Missy's first gold but it wouldn't be her last. She would have more opportunities to see her country's flag raised, and more chances to get the words right when they played the national anthem. "I finally got one. Finally . . . after a whole 17 years," said Missy about her gold medal moment.

Always thinking of others, the Olympian took to the airwaves to express her joy over winning a gold medal. "I am so grateful for everything that has happened. God has blessed me with so much. Thank you so much for all the love and support!" said Missy to her Twitter fans.

"Pretty" is how Missy described her newly-earned medal. It's a good thing she thought the medal was so pretty because it would have to be enough to sustain her upbeat attitude for her next events. Coming in 4th in the 200m freestyle, Missy missed a bronze medal. Undaunted, Missy continued on, getting another gold medal in her next event—this time in the 4x200m

Missy wipes a tear from her face during the medal ceremony for the Women's 100m backstroke on day 3 of the London 2012 Olympic Games.

Adam Pretty/Getty Images

freestyle relay. Missy swam the relay with swimmers Dana Vollmer, Allison Schmitt, and Shannon Vreeland. Missy was the lead swimmer jumping to an early lead, but falling to third place by the time she handed off to her teammate. Missy is a team player and she cheered her teammates on from the pool deck. And her team came through, not only winning the gold, but also setting an Olympic record with a time of 7:42.92.

People began to wonder if she could keep her energy up for the rest of her races. "I'm only 17," responded Missy in an *ESPN.com* article. "There's no such thing as fatigue." Missy proved her statement true when she turned in another stellar performance, not just by winning another gold medal, but also by setting a world record in the 200m backstroke. Her time of 2:04:06, broke a record that had stood since 2009.

"In that last 25m, I knew I was giving it everything I had because I couldn't feel my arms and legs and I was just trying to get my hand to the wall as fast [as] I could," Missy told *ESPN.com*. The next closest swimmer was Russia's Anastasia Zueva, who was a body length behind.

This made four Olympic medals, three of them gold. There was still time for more, and there was no slowing her down. Missy had one more race to go; her last race would be that Saturday. Her week of record-number swimming events would be coming to an end and her first Olympic experience would soon be fading into history. Just one more race.

Missy teamed up again to race in the 4x100m medley relay. As the lead-off swimmer, Missy swam her specialty—the backstroke. She took off at a world record pace. Her fellow swimmers were Rebecca Son, Dana Vollmer, and Allison Schmitt. The women powered through the race swimming the breaststroke, the butterfly, and the freestyle. When the first swimmer hit the touchpad at the end of the race, it was Allison Schmitt for the US who had set a world record at 3:52:05. Missy Franklin and her teammates had won another gold medal.

Four gold medals and a bronze was a pretty good haul for a 17-year-old who planned on returning to high school for her senior year in the fall. At least that was the idea. But the media was going crazy asking the question that was on everyone's mind: Would Missy go pro? There was even some question as to whether she could keep her bonus money from the Olympics, and still be an amateur—making her eligible to compete in college. The answer was a yes—and a no.

She received and was able to keep $100,000 for each gold medal in her individual events—the 100m backstroke and the 200m backstroke. She also shared in $210,000 in bonuses from the other two gold medals and the bronze from her relay events. The one thing she could not receive was a $50,000 bonus from USA Swimming for her world-record swim in the 200m backstroke. Missy still took home a sizeable amount of money—about $225,000—but not as much as she could have if she had sponsors.

"Right now, I'm still very set on swimming in college, but my decision has become a lot harder," said Missy in an *NBC TODAY* interview following her Olympic victories. Now that she had become a winning Olympian, there was the opportunity for even more cash. There were pros and cons to consider. "Turning down this amount of money is unheard of. I mean, it's absolutely absurd. It's an amazing opportunity," Missy told *TODAY.com*.

With God-given skills like Missy had, going to college meant getting a full-ride scholarship for swimming, no matter where she chose to go. This meant Missy could still swim and not worry about the financial burdens of college. Her parents, always supportive of her, left the decision up to her. Yet, as parents, they had to make sure their daughter was clear about her choices. Her father admitted that Missy was on a college path unless "some horrendous amount of corporate money" was thrown at her. If that did happen, according to Dick Franklin in the *Denver Post*, they would sit her down to explain how that money could be her children's education, or a house when she got married. Her parents also knew the money would still be there for at least two to three more years if she didn't go pro right away—something Dick knew from his corporate experience working for athletic giants Reebok and Head. Missy's star power would still be there and Rio 2016 would be the new goal.

"She's good for at least two more Olympics," said Dick to the *Post*.

Teri McKeever, Missy's Olympic coach, felt the same way, as she explained to the *Denver Post*. "Missy and her family have to look at their options and what's important. Her first responsibility is to Missy Franklin, what makes her happy, and it's not to US Swimming. I would tell anybody that," said McKeever.

In a *Sunday Sports Extra* interview Missy summed up her intentions. "I'm 17 years old and I don't want to make swimming my job yet. It isn't about the money. It's not what it's about. I think that what I'm going to get swimming in college for a college team, and competing in NCAA championships, is priceless."

Sometimes all that glitters is not gold. For Missy, the true treasure was in remaining a normal teenager and in returning home to a normal life. Her heart was in swimming and in getting an education. They meant more to her than the money she could get, and all the things money could buy. And no matter what she decided, she knew her parents and friends would stand by her. So it was back to 5:00 a.m. swim practices and the world of a high school senior, even if she was a gold medal Olympian.

Chapter 10

Home Again

Could any of this be real? Could Missy Franklin, who just four years before missed qualifying for the 2008 Olympics, now be headed home from London with five Olympic medals? YES! It was real. But in an interview with *ESPN The Magazine*, Missy said it seemed insane, like she had made the whole thing up. But there's nothing like seeing to believe. "When I pull my medals out at the airport, I sort of sit back and realize, I'm taking an Olympic gold medal through security. And it's *my* Olympic gold medal."

After winning five Olympic medals—four of them gold, at just 17—what do you do next? So many young sports superstars turn pro, leaving school behind to follow the money and more stardom. But if you're Missy Franklin, you go back home as a superstar. And you go back to school, business as usual.

It has been estimated that Missy could have made millions of dollars in endorsements almost immediately.

But for Missy, life was about being a normal teenaged girl. That meant high school classes, dances, proms, and friends. But first there would be a hero's welcome home. When Missy arrived at the airport in Denver after the London Olympics, she was greeted by US flags lined up on both sides of the plane by airport ground personnel, who were also waving flags. The airport terminal was decorated with balloons, streamers, and supporters of the new Olympian, as described in the *Dailycal.org*. Missy Franklin had officially hit the big time.

Missy hit late night TV talk shows, morning news shows—all kinds of programs and events. But most important for her, she made it back to school. School was where her heart was. She was looking forward to getting back to her classmates and her teammates on the Regis Jesuit swim team. She was looking forward to helping them win a state championship title. She had done everything along the way to keep her amateur status so she could continue to compete as an amateur on the high school level. This was about living out her plans like any other teenager.

But some didn't see it that way. Some looked at the swim sensation and asked, why? Why would you return to high school, to compete on your high school's swim team, when you have already beaten the best on the world stage at the Olympics?

The answer was always there. Missy wanted to go to college and be able to compete on the college level as well. But first, she needed to finish out her senior year of high school. And that meant competing on her high school team to help them win a championship.

Missy's parents spoke with her about her choice. They let her know that the money she could make from turning professional would be enough to take care of her *and* her kids. They wanted her to consider all of her options. But Missy wanted to continue living the life of an average teenager and that meant returning to her hometown of Centennial, Colorado, and her high school in Aurora where she would swim right next to the teammates she had grown to know and love.

But the world couldn't get enough of Missy, and fans from her home state were no different. Soon after her return to the US, an event was planned for Colorado's Olympians at Centennial Center Park, with Governor John Hickenlooper welcoming them. Of course, Missy was there.

"This is so awesome," Missy told her audience. "I missed you so much. Going and getting the gold is awesome, but the support we get from Colorado, that's what makes it worth it."

Three weeks later Missy was out on the football field, acting as honorary captain of the Denver Broncos. She was at midfield for the coin toss when the Broncos faced off against the Pittsburgh Steelers. "It's an incredible honor, and I'm very, very blessed I'm able to do this," said Missy to the *Post*.

Missy also swung by the *Tonight Show* with Jay Leno. She had a cameo on the television show *Pretty Little Liars*. She volunteered with the Arthur Ashe Kids' Day—an event with special meaning since her father had worked with tennis legend Arthur Ashe years before.

Missy connected with another tennis legend—Novak Djokovic when she played doubles with him in a mock tennis match just before the US Open.

She was on the *Today Show* and *Access Hollywood*. She was the grand marshal of the Fiesta Bowl in Phoenix.

Matt Lauer and Missy Franklin appear on the NBC "Today" show.

Peter Kramer/NBC/NBC NewsWire via Getty Images

She attended the red carpet at the MTV Awards in Los Angeles. Her life was turning out to be everything her parents had been warned about, and then some. They had been repeatedly told that things would be different, and it was proving to be the case. People recognized her. They wanted photos and time with her.

Home life for Missy became filled with letters and packages from fans. Without an agent, Missy relied on her mother to help her with everything coming in. Often letters and packages were sent to her school and to USA Swimming. One fan even sent her flowers and asked her out on a date. Missy being Missy, called him and thanked him for the flowers. She also spent six to seven hours over one weekend responding to mail and autographing photos and mailing them out, all of this at a cost to her parents who paid for the postage. But this was something Missy and her parents didn't mind at all.

"The mail is not overwhelming. It's so exciting," said Missy in a *Denver Post* article. "It's so special for people to take time out of their crazy schedule to write to me. The letters they write are so incredible. It makes this whole thing worth it."

The Olympics obviously didn't mean the end of swimming for Missy. The Games were just a step in what will probably be a long swimming career for her. She swam for both the USA and for her school following the London Olympics. In November of 2012 she swam at the Minneapolis Grand Prix, winning the 200m butterfly, setting a national record in her age group of 17–18 year-old girls; she also won the 50m freestyle and the 100m backstroke. She finished by winning the 200m backstroke and the 100m freestyle. This was the first meet of a six-meet series. The young Olympian was also glad to get back to swimming competitively on the high school level since her five-medal run at the London Olympics.

Even though she was back to swimming and school, Missy still took some time to go to New York to pick up yet another award at the Golden Goggles, USA Swimming's annual awards banquet. Missy picked up the Female Athlete of the Year award and top relay performance from the world-record race in the 4x100m medley she swam with Rebeca Soni, Dana Vollmer, and Allison Schmitt.

In an Associated Press article for *ESPN*, Missy was still fielding questions about her swimming in high school. If anyone who swam in high school would have told her not to swim, "I would absolutely not swim," said Missy in response to the questions and comments about her participation in high school athletics. But she had the support of others—family, friends, coaches, and classmates—and she continued to swim. Yet, it still bothered her that some people thought it wasn't fair.

"It's hard, because I feel like no matter what I do, it's going to be opposed in some way or form. It's hard, but it's life."

Missy's parents also had to deal with parents who thought their daughter shouldn't swim. D.A. Franklin told *espnW* about the time one parent made a special request of her—"talk to Missy to have her not continue so the other girls can have their day to shine, since Missy has so many other opportunities to shine." D.A. Franklin handled this like any mother would. She explained that it was important to Missy to swim with her team—"the girls she knows and loves." D.A. pointed out things that other mothers may not have thought of, such as the fact that Missy's schedule meant she couldn't always do the things that their daughters did, like sleepovers and school dances. "I feel I need to remind people, she misses out on so much, please don't take something else from her."

Life for Missy meant continuing to swim, to do what God had made her to do, and to feel blessed in everything that she was able to achieve. So next up for Missy was the Winter Nationals in Austin, Texas. She won the 200y backstroke and placed second and third in other races. She also won the meet's high point award for women.

In between meets and schoolwork, Missy had opportunities for other adventures—some in the water and some out. One opportunity was the chance to be part of a movie that would encourage others. She was going to spend spring break filming *The Current*, a movie featuring disabled individuals learning how to scuba dive. Missy was the athlete ambassador for the film. The goal of *The Current* was to help disabled individuals get involved in sports and recreation, according to a *Post* article.

The deep-sea diving movie was being filmed in Bimini and was taking Missy's love of the water to a new level. "When you're in the ocean and you're under water, 60–70 feet deep, everything else just doesn't matter," Missy told the *Post*. "It's just so cool to have that feeling, just being able to escape from everything for a while, just go down and see God's creation that a lot of people don't get a chance to see how beautiful it is. And just to have that peaceful time to take it all in."

The movie also included athletes Bethany Hamilton, featured in her own movie, *Soul Surfer*, about her loss of an arm due to a shark attack, and how her faith brought her back to competition; and Paralympics gold medalist Mallory Weggerman, who dove with Missy.

A little closer to home, Missy also took time to visit the Children's Hospital Colorado along with her Colorado Stars swim coach and swim team. Practice had been cancelled so the swimmers could attend a dance party with the patients. Even though Missy had been on television shows and hung out with famous people, she still found time to give back to people in her community.

One day in December of 2012, Missy hung out with a group of kids at the same hospital, just talking to them—telling stories, making jokes, and making them smile. Missy, still not aware of her own star power, told the *Denver Post* that she was afraid the children would be

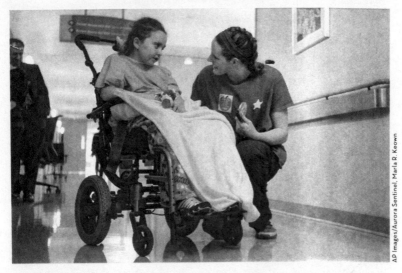

Missy shows Allie Kandt her Olympic Gold Medal, Dec. 13, 2012, at the Children's Hospital in Aurora, Colorado. After visiting patients, Franklin and members of the STARS swim team brought holiday cheer and a variety of dance moves to patients, staff, and families in the hospital's atrium.

expecting another celebrity, like Brad Pitt. But Brad Pitt doesn't have Olympic gold medals, something that Missy was able to hang around the neck of one of the patients.

For all of her efforts to be normal, Missy was racking up more awards and other recognition. Soon after the Olympics, she was named the Colorado Sports Hall of Fame Amateur Athlete of the Year, while Peyton Manning, quarterback for the Denver Broncos, was named the Professional Athlete of the Year.

Being an Olympian had certainly come with its perks. The night before Missy's first swim meet after the Olympics proved to be one of them. She attended a Justin Bieber concert that kept her out past midnight.

The concert came with a special backstage pass to meet "the Biebs", any fan's dream—and Missy was no different. But she still had to get up at 4:45 a.m. the next day for swim practice and a meet.

"Morning practice after the Bieber concert was *not* fun at all," said Missy in an interview with ABC television at her meet. "I've been tired all day." Missy was not only tired, but she was nervous about how she would perform at the meet. She told the *Denver Post* that she was shaking in the locker room. "All my teammates were like, 'What is wrong with you?'" What was wrong was that the excitement and thrill of competing was with her, regardless of the level of competition. She was still the same humble teenager feeling the same excitement and worries as always before a meet.

She didn't need to worry. She was spectacular in all of her events. ABC reporter David Wright asked the coach of the Highlands Ranch Falcons, the team the Regis Raiders competed against that day, if she thought it was fair that Missy was competing against high school swimmers. The Highlands coach, Erica Peharda, saw the competition as a good thing for her swimmers.

"I think it's very great. Missy Franklin is such a great role model for the swimmers," said Peharda. "They look up to her. They were so excited for the meet."

Not only did swimmers from other schools have the chance to say they swam against the world's best female athlete and an Olympian, but they were able to take photos with Missy. It was refreshing to see that even though she had five Olympic gold medals tucked away, she still brought out her signature smile and her winning personality. The fame that might change some didn't have a negative hold on Missy Franklin at all. She was still the girl from Centennial, Colorado who liked to have fun and who loved to swim. And she wasn't going to slack off either. Missy posted a pic of her dark, still workout pool with a tweet that summed up who she is: "Sometimes we complain but there's something beautiful about waking up before everyone to get better at what we love."

For Missy, what she loved to do was swim. The glitter of endorsements and all they would bring was too much like work. Instead, she'd be a teenager and continue to swim for her team, and for the USA. "I have the best friends and family in the world," said Missy in an article in the Catholic Sports Report. "I love being with them and having fun. My friends and I do all the usual high school activities including going to dances, out to see movies, and shopping."

Missy wanted to "make the sport better and definitely not take away from it at all." Missy was once again addressing the controversy over her swimming at the high school level. In an interview with the *Denver Post*, Missy acknowledged her star power and how she could easily pull attention away from other swimmers. She also admitted one thing that made the decision to continue to swim for her high school so hard was the comments. But Missy, being Missy, took the high road, concerning her critics. "That's not their fault at all. They're giving their opinion, and I totally understand that. They are concerned I take attention away. It's totally true. I feel so guilty whenever that happens, but I hope the pros outweigh the cons."

The Highlands Ranch swimmers were definitely part of the "pros" in Missy's decision to keep swimming. They were excited about swimming against her, not to mention the added attention they received when the media showed up to cover Missy's first swim meet following her Olympic success. One Highlands Ranch swimmer, Shawna Doughten, said that she was encouraged when she swam against Missy. She told the *Denver Post*, "She makes you think anyone can do it. It was a lot more fun than a regular meet." This was what swimming was supposed to be about. Fun.

Another Highlands Ranch swimmer, Sydney Merritt, admitted to the *Post* that she had always wanted to see Missy swim and that she wasn't a distraction. "No way. It's really cool," said Merritt.

Chapter 11

Senior Year

Missy stayed at Regis Jesuit through her senior year, but it wasn't an easy choice. She struggled with her decision to either go back to swimming at her high school or take the sponsorships and go pro. In an interview with the *Denver Post*, she talked about that decision and how she prayed to God about it.

"I had a lot of trouble deciding rather [sic] or not to swim high school or not this year 'cause it was really hard for me and I prayed a lot about it and I felt like God was giving me mixed signals the whole time," said Missy. "Some people would come up to me and ask me like, why are you doing this and other people would come up to me and say thank you so much for doing this and kind of back and forth and now I finally realized why I did it."

For Missy it was about being with her teammates and swimming with them for the last time as a team. It would be the last time that she would wear her school's name and colors. "Coming up on the bus today I was thinking what would I be doing if I wasn't on this bus right now? I would be wishing I was on that bus. And I was so happy that I made the decision and that I had the support of the people that I loved and cared about."

Missy's final high school swim meet was against a rival that had their share of state titles. Cherry Creek High School. The Cherry Creek High girls' swim team had lost less than 20 times out of 400 meets in over 38 years. But things could change going up against the proven talent of Missy Franklin. And some parents made their feelings known.

In a *Wall Street Journal* article, one parent made her concerns known. "It's sort of defeating," said one mother of a Cherry Creek swimmer. "She won so many gold medals. I don't know what you're there to prove." Another swimmer expressed her frustration at how Missy "kind of shines above everything." The words were hurtful, but they didn't keep Missy from pursuing her dream, from continuing the path that God had her on.

In the same article, Missy's response back was clear. "The best part of staying amateur is that I am still able to do things like this." Missy was speaking of her eligibility to compete in her high school meets. "I have given up so much for that," said Missy.

It's understandable that swimmers want to achieve greater heights and that parents would want to see their children achieve at a higher level. It is also understandable that Missy Franklin wanted the opportunity to compete as well. As the old saying goes, "a rising tide floats all boats", and in the same regard,

Missy Franklin, swimming strong, could only help to elevate the competition.

In an *ESPN.com* article, Nick Frasersmith, Missy's Regis Jesuit coach, pointed out, "Missy brings incredible talent to us obviously . . . but to be honest, it's probably one of the last reasons I want her back. It's what she brings to the team as far as personality. I think the world has basically gotten to know Missy, what she's about and what she stands for, and that's exactly what she is. What you see is what you get." Frasersmith recognized that Missy had more than raw talent in the water to offer her team. The ability to swim well encourages others to *do* better, but her personality encourages others to *be* better. Frasersmith went on to say, "She's a team player through and through. And when she's in the pool racing, I know our team wants to step up and swim faster."

Missy also received support from John Koslosky, Regis Jesuit athletic director who recognized Missy's passion for swimming and her desire to be with her teammates one last year. "From a swimming standpoint, does she really need it? Probably not. But as for the human part . . . you only go to high school once."

Missy finished out her year as a swimmer for the Regis Jesuit Raiders. She and her teammates won the Class 5A state championship, and for her part Missy set state and national records—winning the 200y individual medley in 56.85 seconds. She set a state record in the 500 freestyle. Her high school swim career included eight individual state championships. At the end of it all Missy knew who to thank.

"I've had so many wonderful experiences and I can't thank God enough," she told *ESPN.com*.

Missy, third from left, and Regis Jesuit High School swimmers jump into the pool after winning the 5A Colorado State Championship in 2013.

Before the end of her senior year, Missy received yet another award—the 2012 James E. Sullivan Award, given to the country's top amateur athlete by the Amateur Athletic Union (AAU). According to their website, the award is "based on the qualities of leadership, character, sportsmanship, and the ideals of amateurism, the AAU Sullivan Award goes far beyond athletic accomplishments and honors those who have shown strong moral character." It is described as the "Oscar" of sports awards.

"This award means a lot to me because of how much I've given up to be amateur," Missy told the *Denver Post*. So who was the last swimmer to win that award? Michael Phelps.

AAU president Henry Forrest described Missy as one of the "best and the brightest" amateur athletes pursuing her dreams. He also noted her character and leadership in the classroom and community. For Missy that meant keeping a 4.0 grade point average while working with a long list of groups including Multiple Sclerosis Association of America, Make-A-Wish Foundation, Stand Up 2 Cancer, and the Denver Children's Hospital.

Somehow she was able to stretch herself, give more, and continue to dig deeper—making morning practices while still taking the swim world by storm.

Missy had reached the big time while still in high school, but soon she would be leaving her home state and her home swim team to swim for her Olympic coach who just happened to be the coach for the Cal Bears. Even though her future was right in front of her, Missy acknowledged all that the Colorado Stars and coach Todd Schmitz had done for her.

"I wouldn't have a career without him," Missy told the *Denver Post*. "Every coach has something about him that makes him special. Todd and I have a relationship that's special in itself." There would be no problem for Missy to go back to swim for Schmitz—but for now she would be looking forward to the next phase of her life.

Chapter 12

Bieber Fever

Nothing says teenager more than being a "Bielieber." Like many young females in the world in 2012, Missy Franklin was a huge Justin Bieber fan. She could often be seen on pool decks dancing by herself to the ever-playing music. You could bet she would be grooving if a Justin Bieber tune came over the loudspeaker.

In a *Today Show* interview after the Olympics, Missy spoke with Matt Lauer. He brought up the Justin Bieber infatuation the young swimmer had. In response to Lauer's comment about what happens with Justin Bieber when you win at the Olympics, the 17-year-old smiled and said, "He notices you."

Missy and Bieber, a fellow Canadian, (Missy has dual citizenship) spoke through the Twittersphere, the young pop star known affectionately as "the Biebs" tweeted, "Heard @FranklinMissy is a fan of mine. now im a fan of hers too CONGRATS on winning Gold #muchlove."

What teenage girl wouldn't get excited to receive a message and hashtag like that from an artist she admired from afar? Missy was no different. When she saw the tweet, she had to respond. Who wouldn't?

She retweeted what he said and added, "I just died. Thank you."

Missy's parents, in a *Today Show* interview, said their daughter sent them a text in all caps (nothing like shouting at your parents when you are excited). It read, "CAN YOU BELIEVE IT!"

The mutual admiration between Missy and Justin continued and after she picked up four gold medals and her bronze, Bieber had a little something extra waiting for her when she got home. He sent her a huge care package brimming with T-shirts, posters, CDs—everything Missy would need to make her the ultimate Bieber fan—a true "Belieber." Missy's mom had the Bieber swag displayed like Christmas on a table.

"It was really sweet of him," said Missy in an interview in *The Post Game*. She quickly took to Twitter to thank the young pop star for his generosity. "Huge shout out to @justinbeiber for sending me all this amazing stuff! Thank you so much! Can't wait for the concert!" Most fans would have to settle for being the happiest girl in the world after getting a personal tweet from Justin Bieber. But Missy had the good fortune to have Justin as a fan. She was even more fortunate that she'd get the chance to meet with him at one of his concert venues. But first, there was the business of the Bieber-swag sent to her.

Missy was quick to remember the pledge she had made to herself—to remain eligible to compete in swimming at the college level. That meant one thing.

Because of NCAA college eligibility rulings, the gifts would probably have to go back. "But it was considered a form of special treatment that could have jeopardized my amateur status. I've given up way too much and sacrificed too much to keep a Justin Bieber T-shirt and lose it all. So I sent it back."

D.A. Franklin reached out to the NCAA to get a decision about keeping the care package, but to be on the safe side she sent it back. As it turns out, Missy could have kept the package and proudly sported all the Bieber-related material while listening to Bieber music. What Bieber did in sending her the swag-package was no different than what he had done for other fans. So, while it had felt special—so special that Missy feared it might get her in trouble with the NCAA—she would have been able to keep it. Her decision to send it back at the time was wise however. The cost of her being able to swim in college was certainly more than the cost of giving up the Bieber souvenirs.

Even though she didn't keep the souvenirs, Missy had good memories from attending a Justin Bieber concert and meeting him in person. She had a chance to check out his backstage digs, costumes, even take a spin on his Segway. And of course there were photo ops—a smiling Missy with her gold medals around her neck and the Biebs at her side.

But the shine on Bieber would not last. In a year's time Bieber had been making the headlines often and not for positive reasons. There had already been rumors of him making questionable choices. While many kids could look the other way while their idol was acting inappropriately, Missy spoke up. It may have been hard to admit that her favorite singer wasn't living up to who she thought he was, but she took a public stance. "I don't agree with all of his life decisions lately, so I've moved on a little from that," said Missy in an *SBNation* article.

Missy realized that it was time for her to put some distance between herself and Justin Bieber, and most importantly his activities. Missy Franklin has always known who she is and what she wants. Bieber was no longer "it."

Chapter 13

Swim On

While her high school swimming career was finished, Missy wasn't done with swimming. There would be more races between her high school state championship and the time she would put her college's swim cap on.

Missy continued to do what Missy does best—win. The Arena Grand Prix series, in Florida, is where she enjoyed her first meet after her high school swimming career ended. Missy took home medals in the 100m back-stroke, placing first; a second in the 200m freestyle, and a first in the 200m backstroke at that event. The biggest difference for her was that she was also experiencing what she called "amazing events" on the weekend. In a *Denver Post* article Missy compared herself to the once-famous television show and its famous namesake, *Hannah Montana*, getting the chance to be "a normal high school student during the week", and on the weekend becoming this celebrity swimmer rubbing elbows with stars like Leonardo DiCaprio at events like the Golden Globes.

She also went on to be the 2012–2013 overall winner for female swimmers of the series that took place in several cities around the country.

Other accolades awaited Missy. She was named one of Colorado's women of influence, and she was inducted into the Colorado Sports Hall of Fame as the amateur athlete of the year. She received a tribute from the state senate and house at the Colorado Capitol. Some athletes would have been satisfied to rake in the millions of dollars. Missy may have missed out on the money, but she wasn't missing out on the recognition for what she did, both as a swimmer and as a person who gave back to her community as often as she could.

This involvement in her community gave Missy a chance to meet Britain's Prince Harry when he took part in the festivities surrounding the 2013 Warrior Games. This competition was between the United States and Great Britain, and included "wounded, ill, and injured military personnel" according to the *Denver Post*. Missy was part of the flame-lighting ceremony signaling the start of the Games. The event even gave Prince Harry a chance to sing *Happy Birthday* to Missy. How many 18-year-olds wouldn't love being serenaded by Prince Harry?

Missy's May birthday signaled another major event in her life—the end of the school year and graduation. After graduation, she would be heading to California for college. Not very many college freshman can pack Olympic medals along with their high school memorabilia. But Missy had done it her way and she was proud of her accomplishments both in and out of the water.

"I think it's such a vital part of growing up, such a huge thing for me," Missy told the *Associated Press*. "My parents and I put so much emphasis on just staying normal. I wanted those experiences. I don't want to look back 10 years from now wishing I had done my senior year of high school, wishing I had gone to my prom, wishing I had experienced those things. The people we meet, the experiences we go through, that's what makes us the people we are, the people we are growing into. This is our time to make mistakes, to learn from them, to learn to shine. It's such a beautiful time in your life."

Her words sounded like something coming from a very mature young lady. She had accomplished so much while the world watched her, yet she tried to remain true to herself. Her next step would be to get a taste of college life in the time leading up to the 2016 Olympics in Rio. She had two more years of the "sweet life" as an amateur, doing all the things that a normal college student would do now. Then it would be off to the pros. In an *AP* article, Missy explained the reason for her timing:

"If I do all four years of college that would be the biggest financial mistake of my life. As much as I would love to do four years, in terms of myself, my welfare, my family's welfare, that wouldn't be the smartest decision." Missy vowed to finish her college degree, just not as an amateur athlete. In the meantime, she was happy to continue to swim, win, break records, and repeat.

Missy collected four wins at the US National Championships in Indianapolis, Indiana in June. Next on her schedule was the World Championships in Barcelona, Spain. Missy went into the competition with all the confidence of an experienced Olympic swimmer, even though she admitted to initially feeling a little different.

It's not every day that you see a 6'1" teenage girl. Initially it was difficult for her, being so much taller than all the boys. But eventually she realized that her height and build was working to her advantage as a swimmer, appropriately nicknamed "Missy the Missile." She'd take this advantage with her to Barcelona where she would compete in eight events. She started out the championships with a gold medal in the 400m freestyle relay where she was the leadoff swimmer. Missy had spent some time between the Olympics and the World Championships working on her freestyle and it showed.

Missy ran into a little trouble when she qualified for the 100m backstroke. A bad push-off from the wall threw her off, but not enough to keep her out of the finals. Her right slipping caused her to just go straight down. She corrected that issue by the final and was able to swim away with a gold medal in the 100m backstroke, quickly followed up by setting the second-fastest time in the 200m freestyle semi-finals. The races were within an hour of each other, but this was something Missy was used to and comfortable with. "It's tough, but it's fun," Missy told the *Associated Press*.

Fun turned into victory when Missy picked up another gold medal in the 200m freestyle final. She also snagged gold in the 200m backstroke, the 800m freestyle relay, and the 400m medley relay. That made six golds and another unique distinction. Not only had she topped the number of gold medals she won at the Olympics, she had won more gold medals than any other female swimmer competing at a world championship.

Once again Missy was the leadoff swimmer, swimming her signature backstroke. Before the race she

Wang Lil/Xinhua/Landov

Missy shows her gold medal during the awards ceremony for the women's 200m backstroke final at the 2013 FINA World Championships in Spain.

encouraged her teammates to just go out and do their best and have fun. Her mantra worked. Their winning time of 53.23 was almost two seconds faster than second-place finisher, Australia.

The six medals from Barcelona and her previous three gold medals from the World Championships in Shanghai gave her nine world titles. This was more than any other female swimmer.

Chapter 14

Golden Bears

Many high school students dream of going to college. Young Olympian Missy Franklin was no different, even though the rest of the world may have thought it should be otherwise. As a high school senior, Missy had already achieved what so many other athletes had only dreamed of—a trip to the Olympics. And what's better than a trip to the Olympics, a chance to represent your country? Winning not just a *medal*, not just a *gold* medal, but *four* gold medals and a bronze. For some it would be easy to make the decision to skip college altogether, with prize money and millions of dollars in sponsorships. But that wasn't for Missy.

Reaching her next goal of being part of a college team was just on the horizon for Missy. She had been looking at the University of Georgia, University of Southern California, University of Texas, and the University of California, Berkeley. If Missy chose the University of California at Berkeley, she would be right back with her Olympic Coach

Teri McKeever, and she already knew what it would be like to swim for her. "A lot of athletes don't get that opportunity before they go to college, so I'm really blessed," said Missy in a *Post* article.

Missy knew the University of California, Berkeley was the place for her from the moment she checked into the Claremont Hotel in Berkeley while on a college visit. She asked her parents, "Is it bad that I haven't even been on campus yet and I already know I'm coming here?" Franklin said in an *espnW.com* article. "I knew it in my heart the whole time."

She let the world know in Missy fashion—with a tweet. "Committed to swim at Cal Berkeley! I am officially a baby Golden Bear . . ." The excitement about her decision came through her tweet, but it didn't compare to the way she told her former Olympic and soon-to-be college coach. Missy did it with a little flair and a lot

Missy sports her Golden Bear attire.

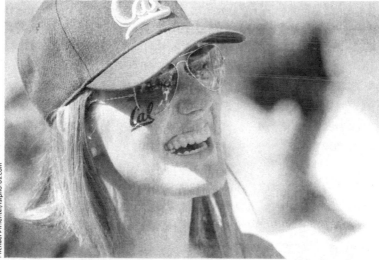

Michael Pimentel/isiphotos.com

of fun. She gave Teri McKeever a phone call the coach may never forget.

McKeever was at a football game at Memorial Stadium when her phone rang. Caller ID told her who it was, but she didn't want to deal with the fact that Missy might be telling her she wasn't attending Cal. She let the call go to her voicemail. Then she got another call from associate head coach Kristen Cunnane who said that Missy needed to talk to her.

Missy decided to have some fun with the call. She drew it out by telling the coach she had made a decision and then she began thanking her for all of her efforts. She also told her that people would be surprised by her decision. McKeever had all but given up on ever having Missy swim for her on the college level. And then Missy said, "I want to come swim for you." Missy had pranked her coach, but in a good way!

McKeever had never really discussed Missy swimming for her when they were at the Olympics. She felt that was inappropriate. But she did visit the swimmer and her family afterward. She knew Missy wanted the team experience of swimming at college. And this was something she would be able to give her.

Another thing UC Berkeley would be able to give Missy was as much of a normal college student life as possible. So before Missy even committed to the university, they talked about safety precautions such as keeping Missy's class schedule a secret. They also talked about handling the media, such as going over media requests. They talked about her being under a "microscope." And they were ready. Now all Missy had to do was move into the dorms and be an official college student.

"I'm so excited," Franklin said about college. "It's scary because it's such a big unknown. I just found out who my roommate is. I literally can't wait because I'm so excited."

Missy had the good fortune of being raised well, by parents that loved, nurtured, and believed in her. They gave her the freedom she needed to discover who she was. It was finally time for her to go out on her own, to be that person at the University of California. But there was one more thing to do before she left for college, and Missy had a dilemma. The Arthur Ashe Kids' Day was scheduled for the day after she had to move into her college dorm—an event stressful in itself. She debated on whether or not to participate in the event. But true to her nature, Missy came through. Her mother, who had taken time away from her career as a doctor to act as Missy's manager, was about to decline Missy's invitation to be part of Arthur Ashe Kid's Day.

" . . . my mom was writing the email and I ran downstairs and said, 'Stop! I have to do this, I have to!'" So Missy honored her commitment, recalling what a good time she had had participating the previous year. And not only was this going to be her first time co-hosting the event, it gave her a way to give back once again.

University of California Berkeley

Established: 1868
Public University
Undergraduate students: 27,126 (2014)
     52% female
     48% male

Graduate Students: 10,455
Full time faculty: 1,620
Mascot: Oski (bear)
Team name: Golden Bears
Olympic gold medals won by alumni: 103
First female students enrolled: 1870
School Colors: Blue and gold
Source: University of California Berkeley

Chapter 15

Freshman on Deck

As much as Missy Franklin wanted to be a normal kid enjoying college life, there were certainly some things that weren't normal about her and those things couldn't be ignored. Like having Olympic gold medals. Like a record-breaking number of medals from the world championships in Barcelona, Spain. Like having a press conference when you start college.

But, Missy being Missy, she entered the press conference with a friendly, "Hi, everybody!" It was Missy's nature to be at ease and to put everyone else at ease with her always-sunny disposition and never-ending smile. She was meeting with the press before her first classes began—explaining to them the joys of moving into her dorm and meeting her roommate.

There would be "regular" college stuff for Missy to experience like fun dance classes (maybe to throw in some new steps on the pool deck). And she had the chance to experience a real California earthquake. But

University of California women's swimming & diving head coach Teri McKeever, left, gestures beside California freshman Missy Franklin during a 2013 news conference.

she would be the one shaking up the world as she continued to swim, this time for Cal. She would also continue doing interviews for the media. This was what it was to be Missy Franklin—super busy but with a positive attitude. Her coach Teri McKeever called it her "new normal." New normal would also include having the swimmers turn off the location applications on their cell phones. Missy would also have to be careful posting pictures (like normal college kids) about things as simple as where they were eating. Measures had to be taken to give the swim sensation as much of a normal college life as possible without media coverage of everything she was doing.

Missy found her classes to be challenging, maybe more so than she expected. Yet she loved it, along with swim practice and competing at the college level. And like many new college students, Missy missed her dog

Ruger and her parents. Missy tried to call her mom daily and Skype and FaceTime every couple of days. It's in those moments she got to see her dog.

"That's been hard for me to realize, that I may not ever live with my parents again," said Missy in an interview with *The New York Times*. Yet, the freshman swimmer still felt college was the best decision ever, despite the growing estimates of millions of dollars left on the table from lost endorsements.

Money is not everything, and Missy made that clear. One of her happiest moments was when she put on a Cal cap and swam at her first home meet. She won the 100y backstroke and assisted her team in a 400 medley relay. For Missy, it had always been about team.

"College swimming is really about the team—even when you're swimming an individual event—you're getting points for the team," Missy explained in a question

Missy hugs and kisses her dog, Ruger.

Jonathan Newton/The Washington Post via Getty Images

and answer session covered in the *Denver Post.* "You win as a team, lose as a team. I have this whole group of girls behind me no matter what happens. I knew that would make me happier and will take me further than any endorsements."

She continued to compete and to be recognized for her efforts, including being named Sportswoman of the Year by the Women's Sports Foundation. Missy received the award in October 2013 in New York City, letting the audience know that, "This is one of the most incredible honors I have ever received," according to an *ESPN.com* article. Missy had to take a late night flight after midterms in order to make the event.

Another award presentation was on her agenda—this time from USA Swimming with five Golden Goggles nominations. Missy won for the Relay Performance of the Year along with Natalie Coughlin, Shannon Vreeland, and Megan Romano in the 4x100 freestyle relay at the world championships in Barcelona, Spain.

She still had the life of a college student mashed up against the life of a celebrity. Missy kept student life at the forefront, even missing the Duel in the Pool, held in Glasgow, Scotland her freshman year. The event didn't work with her finals schedule which was much more important to her.

Keeping team first, Missy's performance in the pool helped propel her UC Berkeley team to a Pac-12 conference championship her freshman year. She also won in the 100y freestyle, the 200y freestyle, and the 500y freestyle. Missy's star power carried over to the relays and her team won the 400y free relay, the 800y free relay, and the 400y medley relay. She cemented her dominance at the meet by being named the Pac-12 Swimmer of the Meet. Missy would finish out her freshman year of college, have a summer of swimming, and then it would be on to year two—her final year of college swimming.

Missy Franklin on Social Media

Missy Franklin isn't shy about sharing her love for God with the world through social media. Here are some of her posts on Twitter and Instagram:

- Sometimes your only available transportation is a leap of faith. – Margaret Shephard

- Happy Friday (with a pic – Because he bends down to listen I will pray as long as I have breath. Psalm 116:2)

- Now this is what I call a perfect Tuesday morning. There is nothing more this girl loves than a chai and her Bible.

- "One who is faithful in very little is also faithful in much..." #Luke 16:10

- Inspiration from Bible Study tonight (Missy posted a picture of: To be a Christian means to forgive the inexcusable because God has forgiven the inexcusable in you. C.S. Lewis)

- Happy Birthday Jesus I couldn't think of a more meaningful reason to celebrate with family and the people we hold dearest in our hearts #comeletusadorehhim #lightand lifetoallHebrings

- The perfect way to end my Sunday #2Corinthians (with a pic of her Bible and notebook – her Bible is well-tabbed and highlighted)

- "May the God of hope fill you with all joy and peace in believing, so that by the power of the Holy Spirit you may abound in hope." Romans 15:13 (posted with a pic of a fortune cookie paper that read, "Hope is the best stimulant of life.")
- (pic) The earth is full of the goodness of the Lord. Psalm 33:5
- (pic) Always pray to have eyes that see the best in people a heart that forgives the worst a mind that forgets the bad, and a soul that never loses faith in God.
- Sending so many prayers to my best friend and her beautiful family as they travel to Asia today to go share the love of God with a Christina's girl's orphanage in Kozhhikode. I am so proud of you and can't wait to see all the beautiful things God will use your hands and words to do. Love you always!
- "Life begins at the end of your comfort zone." I am feeling more blessed than I could have thought possible.
- I am so blessed to live in such an incredible place with such incredible people. With every sunrise and sunset I see God's smile. #colorado #nofilter #gonnamissthis
- Thank you SO SO MUCH for all my birthday wishes! God ad blessed me with every one of you and this has by far been the best birthday ever! I've felt so much love and it means the world to me! God is good! Thank you for making my 18th so special!

Find and follow Missy at:

Facebook: facebook.com/MissyFranklinFans

Twitter: @FranklinMissy

Instagram: instagram.com/missyfranklin88

Chapter 16

Pain in the Fast Lane

The unexpected happens when you least expect it. This was no less true for Missy. She had been swimming non-stop since her first competition at the age of five. True to her nickname "Missy the Missile," it seemed that she was on a straight path and nothing could stop her. She had done things that no other female swimmer had done, like winning a record number of gold medals in six events at the FINA World Championships in Barcelona. She had competed in a record number of events at the 2012 Olympics in London. She had won Olympic gold four times and was most proud of her first Olympic medal—a bronze medal. And when she swam she didn't complain about the order of her events. She even missed the opening of the London Olympics so that she would be rested for her first competition. She knew the importance of the moment. Oftentimes her events were very close together, but she was always able to rise up to the challenge. Missy could make it seem easy to go from one race to the next, without a problem and without hesitation.

But this time it was different. Something was wrong. And it frightened her. The world would catch its first glimpse of their "Golden Girl" looking a little less than golden in the moment. Missy was down. And she was in pain.

On August 19, 2014, a video from the Canadian sports network SportsNet surfaced, showing Missy unable to stand without assistance. She was visibly in pain and moved very carefully. The video was taken at a pre-Pan Pacific Championship training, according to a *Swimswam.com* article. She was just two days from the start of the Pan Pacific games that Thursday.

Karen Crouse of the *New York Times* wrote that on that Tuesday, Missy was in the water for a second light practice of the day. Her lower back was already a little tight, according to the *Times* article. When Missy tried to climb out of the water, her back started to spasm. Missy found she couldn't move. This wasn't what she needed at the moment.

"I couldn't put pressure on my back at all. I think even more than the pain, I was terrified," said Missy in the article. As Missy left the area, a person on either side of her could be seen helping her walk out. It was reported that she had to lay in the van in the baggage area because she was in so much pain. It was all she could do to breathe, and her coach, Teri McKeever, had to keep her focused on breathing even if it meant breathing through the pain.

"Coming all the way out here and not being able to swim literally would have just broken my heart," commented Missy in the *Times* article. "I think that's one of the reasons I was so scared at first is because I didn't think I'd be able to."

Missy had the good fortune to have her parents with her during this event, doing what great parents like the Franklins do—lifting up their daughter, encouraging her as much as possible.

The treatment for Missy's back problem included rest along with painkillers, acupuncture, and ice massages. There had never been any reports of back problems before; it appeared to be all new territory for the Olympian. Yet during it all, she kept to her true personality, even tweeting to the world about her back spasms. True to form, she let her fans know that she was "already feeling better."

The next morning, Missy did not go to the Gold Coast Aquatic Center with her team, nor did she attend a scheduled news conference along with other members of the US team. Instead she stayed at the hotel. Missy was able to swim at a local pool "with minimal discomfort," according to an Associated Press article picked up by *ESPN.com*. The swim was to test her back. Missy was looking forward to swimming in the 200m freestyle and the 100m backstroke. Whether she would be able to compete or not remained to be seen, and ultimately would be decided on the day of the race.

Back spasms can be excruciating, and can take out even the most physically, well-prepared athlete. But Missy wasn't ready to give up. On Thursday, the opening day of the competition, Missy warmed up in the pool. She was ready to compete.

Coach McKeever and Missy decided that she would do both races. In *Swimming World News* Missy explained her decision to swim, in spite of the pain and the fear of injury. "I figured, 'Heck, why not! I'm just going to go for it. We'll see what happens. I have some really tough competition, but regardless of what happens, I want to know that I went out there and I fought for it. If I do that, then I'll be able to sleep regardless of the time.'"

Her first event was the 200m freestyle. She didn't go as fast as she would have liked, coming in third among her teammates. She needed to come in second because only two per country could advance to the final. Missy would have to swim in a consolation race.

Her next test would be the 100m backstroke. She had won the 100m backstroke at the London Olympics in 2012. But this was a different stage and a different time, under different circumstances. She rose to the occasion however, coming in as the fastest American and advancing to the finals.

"After this morning I really felt like I could tough it out and do both. Even though there was still that little bit of discomfort, I thought, 'Why not? I'm just going to go for it,'" said Missy in the *Times* article.

Missy won her 200m consolation final with a time of 1:56.04 setting a meet record until Katie Ledecky set a faster time in the next heat. The important thing was that Missy was able to better her own time, and even if momentarily, set a meet record. She was able to do this because, in spite of the pain, she didn't give up.

Missy still had one more race, the 100m backstroke. This was *her* event. She didn't win it. But she did finish. She came in third at the international competition. With setbacks just two days before the competition, she was able to tough it out and see it through to the end.

"I'm really proud of myself, and honestly, it has nothing to do with my times, it has nothing to do with my places, but just getting out and kind of fighting back against life right now," said Missy in the *Times* article.

She reached out to her fans in a more detailed post to her Instagram account:

> *"Definitely not the meet I expected going in, but I am truly learning to trust in God's timing and His plan. I have learned so much, and am thrilled to have qualified for Worlds next summer in my four individual events and three relays. Excited to get back to Berkeley and take some time to recover. Thank you for all your endless support and words of encouragement these past several days."*

The ability to fight against all types of adversity, and maybe pain is the worse one, is what it means to be an Olympian. Missy Franklin, though not a winner in her events at the Pan Pacific championships, proved that winning is not always about touching the wall first. It's about perseverance, and it's about faith.

God's Perfection

To watch Missy Franklin glide in the water to victory is to watch near perfection. This swimmer is built in every way for the sport—from her head to her toes. God's hand can be seen in her development into a world-class swimmer. She stands at 6'1" tall (the average height for an American female is 5'4" according to the CDC). Length is advantage in swimming from entering the water to slicing through it much like a missile, which Missy has been compared to. She has a wingspan, from fingertip to fingertip, of 6'4". She has large hands measuring 8.5 inches from fingertip to wrist. A *Washington Post* infographic compared them to a large canoe paddle, allowing her to exert more force and propel herself farther and faster with each stroke.

Missy wears a size 13 shoe. Her father has likened her feet to built-in flippers; they are very flexible—called plantar flexion, an advantage in swimming fast—giving her "lift" force. Initially, the young swimmer was so bothered by having such large feet (a size 13 for women is like a size 11 in a man's shoe) that she would wear the same size shoe, even after she had outgrown them. But when she was just ten years old, a coach told her that "all his best swimmers had big feet." According to Franklin's mother, after that Missy would ask for larger sizes.

SUMMER GAMES · London 2012

A big backstroke

Missy Franklin won the women's 100-meter backstroke final, her first gold medal and second medal in London, after winning bronze in the 4x100m freestyle relay.

Physical attributes give Franklin an edge on competition

Very tall, with a wide wingspan
6'-1" (1.85 m) tall with a
6'-4" (1.9 m) wingspan

Big feet provide a strong kick
Wears size 13 shoes

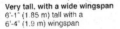

Missy Franklin

Age 17
Weight 165 lb. (79 kg)

Personal Will be a high school senior in Aurora, Colo., in the fall

Big hands for strong pull
8.5 in. (21.6 cm) from wrist to fingertip

Good technique on flip turns
Times the flip so her feet touch the wall at the right time

Wall
Strong push off the wall
Strong legs give her good thrust

© 2012 MCT
Source: USA Swimming
Graphic: Judy Shear, Matt Moody, Los Angeles Times

© Tribune News Service. All Rights Reserved. Reprinted with permission

Her upper body is broad and tapered. This form reduces water resistance. Her larger body also supports strong lungs, heart, and muscle, all advantages in the water. She has strong shoulders which allow her to maximize thrust and overcome drag, key components of fluid dynamics according to a science360.gov video. Dr. Timothy Wei, dean of the college of engineering at the University of Nebraska—Lincoln defined thrust as the motion that pushes the swimmer forward and drag is the resistance of the water to the motion of the body.

Swimmers like Missy have to deal with three types of drag: frictional drag when friction pulls the water next to the body along with her, making it harder to move forward; pressure drag—as the water moves around her head and body and reattaches to her feet—a pressure difference is created between the front and back—a force that can push her backwards. Wave drag happens when water is pushed in front of the swimmer creating a "wave barrier" which the swimmer has to swim over. Missy uses thrust to push through those three types of drag. She counters these different drags by cupping her hands and pushing the water behind her, and by kicking hard with her large feet, much like flippers. She also uses a technique called streamlining—minimizing her contact with the water—making her body as long and narrow as possible to move through the water. Streamlining and thrust counter drag, and Missy is unique and dynamic in using those two techniques with the body God gave her.

"Being in the water just is so natural for me and it comes like walking on land. I absolutely love what I'm doing and I think it gives me an advantage," says Missy.

Chapter 17

The End is the Beginning

This was it. Her college career as a swimmer was coming to an end, but Missy vowed to continue her studies at a later date, until she earned her degree. The only thing left was the NCAA Swimming and Diving Championships in March 2015. Missy had already let the world know she would only go to college and compete in swimming on the college level for two years. She stuck to the plan that she and her family had laid out after she came back from London. Having a plan and following it made it easier for her to make the move to leave college after two years.

Even though she was leaving early, Missy had packed quite a bit into the two years she was at Cal Berkeley. She helped her team capture their conference championship. This was their second straight Pac-12 Championship title. This meant two titles with Missy swimming for the team two years in a row, setting an American record in the 200y freestyle her freshman year, and being named Pac-12 Freshman of the Year.

Missy's role in the 2015 Pac-12 Championship included her contribution to an American record in the 800y freestyle relay. Their time of 6:50.18 also set a school record, US Open, and NCAA record. Missy also dominated in the 200y individual medley and the 200y freestyle. She also took the 200y backstroke.

The Cal Bears' performance was just the beginning. Now it was time to move on to the NCAA tournament. But before that tournament Missy would hear of a loss in the swimming world.

French swimmer and Olympic gold medalist Camille Muffat died along with nine other people in a helicopter crash in Argentina on March 9, 2015. Muffat was in a helicopter with other athletes participating in a reality television show—among them Olympic bronze medalist boxer Alexis Vastine and sailor Florence Arthaud. The French swimmer had won a gold in the 400m freestyle and a silver in the 200m freestyle at the 2012 Olympics in London. She followed that up with a bronze in the 200m freestyle at the 2013 World Championships. Muffat retired in the summer of 2014 but had been a top competitor of Missy Franklin's. Soon after word of the tragedy spread across the world, Missy reached out to her fans through Twitter.

"Truly can't believe the news about Camille Muffat," began Missy's tweet. "My thoughts and prayers go out to her friends and family and all those affected."

Less than two weeks later Missy was swimming at what would be the last swim meet of her college career. This one weekend in Greensboro, North Carolina would signal the end of a chapter and the beginning of a new one. Missy wanted to end this chapter on a high note, helping her Cal Berkeley Golden Bears to an NCAA Championship.

Missy lead off her run at the Championship by winning the 200y individual medley on Thursday, March 19. She wasn't finished. On Friday, she followed up her first win with a win in the 200y freestyle, setting an American record. On Saturday she did it again in her signature event—the 200y backstroke. She also helped the Bears win two relays. Missy's three wins did more than just help her team to win; it also put her on the same level as former UC Berkeley swimmer Natalie Coughlin as the only swimmers to win three championships at an NCAA Championship.

Cal won the overall meet and sent Missy out on top, just as she had wanted and planned.

Missy's hard work was again celebrated when she was named the Muscle Milk Student Athlete of the Week at Cal. Shortly after her stellar performance at the NCAA Championship, Missy was named the 2015 NCAA Swimmer of the Year. She was also named a finalist for the Honda Sports Award for swimming and diving and has since been awarded the prestigious 2015 Honda Cup Award.

The last race of Missy's career meant the beginning of her new life. She would go from the life of swimming on her school's team to swimming for pay. And the pay would be big. First courted by corporations at 15, she managed to hold off, go to the Olympics, win gold, and follow it up with a big win in Barcelona, Spain at the World Championships. If big corporations wanted her at 15, surely they would have something to say at 20 as she prepared for the next Olympics.

In an interview with *espnW.com*, Missy said one of the first things she would do after going pro would be take her parents out to dinner, and pay for it. Her parents were her best friends, still sending her care packages and goodie bags before big events. Most important, they never pressured her to do more than she was ready for or more than she wanted to do.

The Franklins decided to stay in Colorado when everyone else was telling them they should move so Missy could have the best training. In 2012, Missy told ESPN that where she was living was working for her. Her hypothetical question then was, "Why would I ever change that?" Dick and D.A. Franklin listened to their daughter and kept her where she felt the most comfortable. And it was paying off. Mom and Dad were due a nice dinner.

Dick and D.A. Franklin operated as Missy's managers, keeping up with her schedule, her mail, and looking at potential agents. When they had the choice down to two, they left it up to Missy to choose. On Saturday night Missy and her team celebrated their team victory with Italian food. This celebration in North Carolina would be one of her last as a Cal Golden Bear teammate. On Sunday morning Missy was in New York City with her parents. It was time for her to sign on the dotted line. She would have an agent and he would take over much of the work her parents had done. Swimming had always been fun for her, but now it was going to be her job. Endorsements would be coming in.

Missy chose Mark Ervin of WME-IMG, a Beverly Hills, California agency who represented big names in sports such as tennis phenom Maria Sharapova, NFL quarterback Colin Kaepernick, Olympic skier Lindsey

Vonn, and Olympic snowboarder Shawn White. In an Associated Press article, Missy said that she was confident in her choice. "I felt this incredible connection with him," said Missy of Ervin. "I feel like 100 percent we stand for the same things."

These things for Missy include the ability to reach more people. "I can create a platform where I can inspire, reach out and help and encourage. Being a pro athlete gives me a lot of opportunities." Missy spent six hours hashing out these opportunities with her new agent at her family home, according to the *Denver Post*. And then she had to prepare for yet another event—a banquet that next Saturday in Nashville, Tennessee.

Missy was named one of Ten Outstanding Young Americans, an honor bestowed on her by the United States Junior Chamber (Jaycees). Her nomination listed Missy's involvement in "philanthropic efforts"—the time she shared with others such as giving swim lessons to children in Malaysia, spending time at recesses with children in schools in California, and collecting backpacks for American troops to give to Iraqi children to encourage them to attend school.

This award focused on the volunteer work Missy did during her amateur career. It also, without directly saying it, spoke to her huge heart for giving back to others. She had been busy with opportunities she had taken to reach out and encourage others. Now she would be able to continue to do this, while being paid. And school wasn't totally out of the picture. This would be the first time in her life that Missy had the chance to swim full time while taking a lighter load of classes. She wasn't giving up on her degree. Taking classes online would

Missy gives a swimming lesson to local children in Malaysia.

be an option, with the possibility of going back full time sometime after the 2016 Olympics.

Beyond the NCAA Championship, Missy aspired to another goal—to be the most decorated female swimmer of all time. She told *espnW.com* her formula for making that happen: "It's all about goals that are really high for yourself and doing whatever you can to reach them." Missy's "do whatever you can" attitude to reach her goals is what keeps her on everyone's radar when it comes time to hand out awards and medals.

This can-do attitude was part of the 110 percent goal she had set for herself back in 2008. This was the 110 percent that had taken her to the 2012 Olympics. This was the 110 percent that kept her focused on finishing out her high school swimming career, helping the Regis Jesuit Raiders earn a state title, all while maintaining better than a 4.0 grade point average. This is what kept her going through college for two years while still competing internationally.

"Going to college mattered to me for so many different reasons, the main one being my education," said Missy in a statement to *espnW.com*. In leaving college early, Missy didn't feel she was walking away from her education; instead she was preparing for a day when she would no longer be swimming. She was preparing for her future. Most importantly, she was ready for it.

Time spent in college may even have given Missy an edge; she hadn't skipped out on the fun and magic of being a young person. She wasn't missing out on the things that young people her age were doing so she would never look back with regret. Instead, she continued her education, making it a priority. She also continued to compete. This gave her time to mature, time to be able to adjust and to deal with the media blitz that would become her life as a professional swimmer.

The time she spent in college also gave potential sponsors time to see what Missy was made of, both in the pool and out. She proved herself to be as exceptional a person as she is an athlete. In a time when many young athletes and movie stars are out drinking, doing drugs, and displaying other bad behavior, Missy was working on her freestyle stroke, studying for tests, and starring in a documentary with swimmer Kara Lynn Joyce (*Touch the Wall*) about their time leading up to the 2012 Olympics.

Greg Busch, president of Bespoke Sports Entertainment saw Missy's decision to wait to go professional as something that would help her, not harm her. "Whatever she may have given up to go to college the last two years, she'll make up 100-fold," said Busch to *USA TODAY*.

Even Missy's social media presence reflects who she is—a young lady who loves her family, friends, and God. A September 2014 Instagram post displayed a do-it-yourself project on which she painted an empty picture frame, attached string across it, and clipped sayings to the strings. Her post read, "This! I am going to love waking up every day to this [sic] amazing quotes!" Prominently displayed in the middle of the frame is a Bible verse that reads: "Nothing can stop God's plan for your life" Isaiah 14:27.

In June of 2015, Missy signed her first endorsement with Speedo swimwear. In an interview with the *Denver Post*, Missy said, "Speedo is a brand I have trusted since I began swimming." Street & Smith's *Sports Business Daily* reported that Missy will be in ads featuring Speedo competitive swimwear and water-based fitness gear and equipment.

And if you ever travel to Denver by air, you might recognize the voice over the loudspeakers—Missy has recorded a welcome message for the Denver International Airport.

Becoming professional gave Missy an opportunity to do other worthwhile things. For example she was named a Laureus Ambassador. This is the organization that nominated her for a World Sports Award in 2012 and 2014, winning the Laureus Sportswoman of the Year award in 2014. According to a *SwimSwam* article, Laureus Ambassadors work to accomplish the organization's goals.

Missy became another ambassador—this time for USA Swimming Foundation. Missy would be supporting their mission to "Save Lives & Build Champions in the pool and in life," according to their website. The Foundation sponsors the Make A Splash initiative which helps give children an opportunity to learn to swim. The number of non-swimmers in the US is staggering. According to the website, 70 percent of African American children, 60 percent of Hispanic/Latino children, and 42 percent of Caucasian children have little to no swimming ability. "From the first time I became aware of the USA Swimming Foundation, I've been so impressed by its impact to teach children how to swim and learn to be safer around the water," said Franklin.

She is also a supporter of USA Swimming's Building Champions program, which supports the National Team athletes and coaches. National Team members receive a monthly stipend ranging from $1,000 to $3,250. This funding covers the top 12 athletes during 2015–2016, and will go back up to the top 14 athletes during the 2016–2017 season, according to a *SwimSwam* article. For many professional athletes, swimming is their job and endorsements and stipends are their paycheck—what they use to live and take care of themselves.

When Missy made the decision to go pro, she also made the decision to move back to Colorado to swim under her childhood coach, Todd Schmitz. This move surprised many because she would be back swimming with high school kids, instead of the college and adult swimmers she swam with in college. In a *New York Times* article Missy explained that the transition she was going through—from being a college athlete to a professional athlete—was something she wanted her parents to be part of. "For me, it was a lot about family and being able to spend that time with them now."

While one chapter of her life ends, a new one begins. Going pro didn't come with easy victories for Missy. It took seven meets before she came home with a win in an individual race. Missy placed, but not first, in meets in Santa Clara, Calif., and she couldn't pull a first place win at the World Championships. She traveled on to FINA World Cup events in Paris, Hong Kong, Beijing, and Singapore, but she again she went without a first place finish. "You can't hope to develop yourself as a person without those kinds of disappointments as an athlete," said Missy to NBC Sports. "As hard as it is working through that, I think that's been really, really good for me."

Missy's glass-half-full attitude paid off and she took a first place podium spot when she won the 100m backstroke in Minneapolis at the Pro Swim Series in November 2015. "Getting a win under my belt for the first time in quite a while feels really, really good," said Franklin to NBC Sports. Missy took two more first place wins in December when she won at the AT&T Winter National Championships in Federal Way, Washington. She won a national title in the 200m backstroke, and followed that up with a win in the 100m backstroke. She also swam away with a fourth place in the 100m freestyle and a second place in the 200m freestyle.

The Duel in the Pool at the IU Natatorium on the campus of IUPUI in Indianapolis gave Missy another victory—and another record. At the December 2015 meet between the USA and Europe's finest swimmers, Missy set a new US Open record in the 200m freestyle. This victory contributed to Team USA's overall seventh consecutive win against the European All-Stars. "It's so exciting, so awesome for us. It gives us a lot of momentum going into next year," said Missy in an Associated Press interview.

Missy Franklin is living proof of God's word. In an interview on *SwimVortex.com* in 2014, Missy had laid out her plan for how long she might swim. Ideally, she would swim two years in college, something she had been saying all along. Then, as for her professional career, she would swim for a very long time, but as she admitted, no one can make those types of predictions; there are so many factors that can affect them. She also knows she wants to get married someday, have a family, and maybe be a kindergarten teacher. But of course there will always be swimming in her life.

Whatever she does, we know Missy Franklin will have a plan, and that plan will involve God, as Missy relayed in an interview with *Laureus.com*. "I think I'm going to go down the path that God has for me and let everything work out the way it's supposed to."

Missy Franklin: Did You Know Facts

Did you know that the water temperature for competitive swim team training is 82 degrees or less? According to USA Swimming, the ideal air temperature is between 78-80 degrees, and never higher than 82 degrees.

Did you know that the best temperature for drinking water is between 50 and 72 degrees? According to *Prevention* magazine, this is the best temperature for the intestines to quickly absorb the water. You'll be hydrated faster.

Did you know that swim competitions are measured in yards and meters depending on where it is held? According to USA Swimming, short course pools are 25 yards or meters long while long course pools are 50 meters long. The Olympics use the 50 meter length and world records are recorded using 25 and 50 meters. College competitions are generally swum in short course 25 yard pools. Many club pools are 50 meters while many high school pools are 25 yards.

Did you know that Olympic time clocks have to be extremely accurate? "Olympic clocks are 100 times more accurate than a regular stopwatch," according to electrical engineer Linda Milor. When swimmers touch the wall, sensors embedded in the wall "convert the pressure of their touch to an electrical impulse." So when you read the time at a swim competition you are looking at minutes, seconds, and hundredths of seconds.

Swimming Terms–Abridged

Anchor—the final swimmer in a relay. Also a term coaches use for the beginning of all four strokes indicating the "high elbow," "catch," or "early vertical forearm."

Backstroke—one of the four competitive racing strokes, basically any style of swimming on your back. Backstroke is swum as the first stroke in the Medley Relay and second stroke in the IM. Racing distances are 50 yards/meter, 100 yards/meter, and 200 yards/meter (LSCs with 8-under divisions offer the 25 yd back).

Blocks—the starting platforms located behind each lane in a pool. Minimum water depth for use of starting blocks is four feet. Blocks have a variety of designs and can be permanent or removable.

Breaststroke—one of the four competitive racing strokes. Breaststroke is swum as the second stroke in the Medley Relay and the third stroke in the IM. Racing distances are 50 yards/meter, 100 yards/meter, and 200 yards/meter. (LSCs with 8-under divisions offer the 25 yd breast).

Butterfly—one of the four competitive racing strokes. Butterfly (nicknamed "fly") is swum as the third stroke in the Medley Relay and first stroke in the IM. Racing distances are 50 yards/meter, 100 yards/meter, and 200 yards/meter (LSCs with 8-under divisions offer the 25 yd fly).

Championship Meet—the meet held at the end of a season. Qualification times are usually necessary to enter a meet.

Championship Finals—the top six or eight swimmers (depending on the number of pool lanes) in a prelims/finals meet who, after the prelims are swum, qualify to return to the finals. The fastest heat of finals when multiple heats are held.

Closed Competition—swim meet which is only open to the members of an organization or group. Summer club swim meets are considered to be "closed competition."

Club—a registered swim team that is a dues-paying member of USA-S and the local LCS.

Code of Conduct—a code of conduct that both swimmers and coaches are required to sign at certain USA-S/LSC sponsored events. The code is not strict and involves common sense and proper behavior.

Course—designated distance (length of pool) for swimming competition (i.e., long course = 50 meters, short course = 25 yards or 15 meters).

Deadline—the date meet entries must be "postmarked" by to be accepted by the meet host. Making the meet deadline does not guarantee acceptance into a meet since many meets are "full" weeks before the entry deadline.

Deck—the area around the swimming pool reserved for swimmers, officials, and coaches. No one but an "authorized" USA Swimming member may be on the deck during a swim competition.

Dehydration—the abnormal depletion of body fluids (water). The most common cause of swimmers' cramps and sick feelings.

Distance—how far a swimmer swims. Distances for short course are: 25 yards (1 length), 50 yards (2 lengths), 100 yards (4 lengths), 200 yards (8 lengths), 400 yards (16 lengths), 500 yards (20 lengths), 1000 yards (40 lengths), 1650 yards (66 lengths). Distances for long course are: 50 meters (1 length), 100 meters (2 lengths), 200 meters (4 lengths), 400 meters (8 lengths), 800 meters (16 lengths), 1500 meters (30 lengths).

Disqualified—a swimmer's performance is not counted because of a rules infraction. A disqualification is shown by an official raising one arm with open hand above his or her head.

Diving Well—a separate pool or a pool set off to the side of the competition pool. This pool has deeper water and diving boards/platforms. During a meet, this area may be designated as a warm-down pool with proper supervision.

Dryland—the exercises and various strength programs swimmers do out of the water.

Dual Meet—type of meet where two teams/clubs compete against each other.

Electronic Timing—timing system operated on DC current (battery). The timing system usually has touchpads in the water, junction boxes on the deck with hook-up cables, buttons for backup timing, and a computer-type console that prints out the results of each race. Some systems are hooked up to a scoreboard that displays swimmers.

Entry—an individual, relay team, or club roster's event list in a swim competition.

Entry Chairperson—the host club's designated person who is responsible for receiving and making sure the entries have met the deadline.

Entry Fees—the amount per event a swimmer or relay is charged. This varies depending on the LSC and type of meet.

Event—a race or stroke over a given distance. An event equals one preliminary with its final or one timed final.

False Start—when a swimmer leaves the starting block before the horn or gun. One false start will disqualify a swimmer or a relay team, although the starter or referee may disallow the false start due to unusual circumstances.

False Start Rope—a recall rope across the width of the racing pool for the purpose of stopping swimmers who were not aware of a false start. The rope is about halfway on yard pools and about 50 feet from the starting end on meter pools.

Fastest to Slowest—a seeding method used on the longer events held at the end of a session. The fastest seeded swimmers participate in the first heats followed by the next fastest and so on.

Fees—money paid by swimmers for services (i.e. practice fees, registration fee, USA-S membership fee, etc.).

FINA—the international rules-making organization for the sport of swimming.

Finals—the final race of each event.

Flags—pennants that are suspended over the width of each end of the pool approximately fifteen feet from the wall.

Freestyle—one of the four competitive racing strokes. Freestyle (nicknamed "free") is swum as the fourth stroke in the Medley Relay and the fourth stroke in the IM. Racing distances are 50 yards/meter, 100 yards/meter, 200 yards/meter, 400m/500yd, 800m/1000yd, 1500m/1650yd (LSCs with 8-under divisions offering the 25 yd free).

Goals—the short- and long-range targets for swimmers to aim for.

Goggles—glasses-type devices worn by swimmers to keep their eyes from being irritated by the chlorine in the water.

Gun (or Bell) Lap—the part of a freestyle distance race (400 meters or longer) when the swimmer has two lengths plus five yards to go. The starter fires a gunshot (or rings a bell) over the lane of the lead swimmer when the swimmer is at the backstroke flags.

Heats—all of the swimmers entered in the event are divided into heats, or groups of swimmers. The results are compiled by the times swam after all heats of the event are completed.

Illegal—doing something against the rules that is cause for disqualification.

IM—Individual Medley. A swimming event using all four of the competitive strokes on consecutive lengths of the race. The order must be: butterfly, backstroke, breaststroke, freestyle. Equal distances must be swum of each stroke. Distances offered: 100 yards, 200 yards/meters/ 400 yards/meters.

Invitational—type of meet that requires a club to request an invitation to attend the meet.

Jump—an illegal start done by the second, third, or fourth member of a relay team. The swimmer on the block breaks contact with the block before the swimmer in the water touches the wall.

Junior Nationals—a USA-S Championship meet for swimmers eighteen years old or less. Qualification times are necessary.

Kick Board—a flotation device used by swimmers during practice.

Lane—the specific area in which a swimmer is assigned to swim (i.e. Lane 1 or Lane 2).

Lane Lines—continuous floating markers attached to a cable stretched from the starting end to the turning end for the purpose of separating each lane and quieting the waves caused by racing swimmers.

Lap—one length of the course. Sometimes may also mean down and back (2 lengths) of the course.

Leg—the part of a relay event swam by a single team member. A single stroke in the IM.

Long Course—a 50-meter pool.

LSC—local swim committee. The local level administrative division of the corporation (USA-S) with supervisory responsibilities within certain geographic boundaries designated by the corporation. There are fifty-nine LSCs.

Marshall—the official who controls the crowd and swimmer flow at a swim meet.

Meet—a series of events held in one program.

Meet Director—the official in charge of the administration of the meet. The person directing the "dry side" of the meet.

Meters—the measurement of the length of a swimming pool that was built per specs using the metric system. Long course meters is 50 meters, short course meters is 25 meters.

NAGTS——National Age Group Time Standards: the list of "C" through "AAAA" times published each year.

Nationals—USA Swimming National Championship meet conducted in March/April and August.

Natatorium—a building constructed for the purpose of housing a swimming pool and related equipment.

NCAA—National Collegiate Athletic Association.

Non-Conforming Time—a short course time submitted to qualify for a long course meet, or vice versa.

NT—the abbreviation for No Time, it is used on a heat sheet to designate that the swimmer has not swam that event before.

Officials—the certified adult volunteers who operate the many facets of a swim competition.

Olympic Trials—the USA-S sanctioned long course swim meet held the year of the Olympic Games to decide which swimmers will represent the USA on its Olympic team. Qualification times are faster than Senior Nationals.

Pace Clock—the electronic clocks or large clocks with highly visible numbers and second hands, positioned at the ends or sides of a swimming pool so the swimmers can read their times during warm-ups or swim practice.

Paddles—colored plastic devices worn on the swimmers hands during swim practice.

Positive Check In—the procedure required before a swimmer swims an event in a deck-seeded or pre-seeded meet. The swimmer or coach must indicate the swimmer is present and will compete.

Practice—the scheduled workouts swimmers attend with their swim team/club.

Prelims—session of a prelims/finals meet in which the qualification heats are conducted.

Prelims-Finals—type of meet with two sessions. The preliminary heats are usually held in the morning session The fastest six or eight (Championship Heat) swimmers and the next fastest six or eight swimmers (Consolation Heat) return in the evening to compete in the finals. A swimmer who has qualified in the Consolation Finals may not place in the Championship Finals even if their finals time would place them so. The converse also applies.

Pre-seeded—a meet conducted without a bull pen in which a swimmer knows what lane and heat they are in by looking at the heat sheet or posted meet program.

Psyche Sheet—an entry sheet showing all swimmers entered into each individual event. Sometimes referred to as a "heat sheet" or meet program. However, a "heat sheet" would show not only every swimmer in an event, but also what heat and lane they are swimming in.

Pull Buoy—a flotation device used for pulling by swimmers in practice.

Qualifying Times—published times necessary to enter certain meets, or the times necessary to achieve a specific category of swimmer. See "A," "AA" (etc.) times.

Ready Room—a room poolside for the swimmers to relax before they compete in finals.

Recall Rope—a rope across the width of the racing pool for the purpose of stopping swimmers who were not aware of a false start. The rope is about half way on yard pools and about 50 feet from the starting end on meter pools. (same as false start rope)

Referee—the head official at a swim meet in charge of all of the "wet side" administration and decisions.

Relays—a swimming event in which four swimmers participate as a team. Each swimmer completes an equal distance of the race. There are two types of relays: 1) Medley relay—one swimmer swims backstroke, one swimmer swims breaststroke, one swimmer swims butterfly, one swimmer swims freestyle, in that order. Medley relays are conducted over 200 yd/m and 400 yd/m distances. 2) Freestyle relay—each swimmer swims freestyle. Free relays are conducted over 200 yd/m, 400 yd/m, and 800 yd/m distances.

Sanction—a permit issued by an LSC to a USA-S group member to conduct an event or meet.

Sanction Fee—the amount paid by a USA-S group member to an LSC for issuing a sanction.

Sanctioned Meet—a meet that is approved by the LSC in which it is held. Meet must be conducted according to USA Swimming rules. All participants, including coaches, athletes, and officials, must be USA Swimming members.

Seed—assign the swimmers heats and lanes according to their submitted or preliminary times.

Seeding—Deck Seeding: swimmers are called to report to the clerk of the course. After scratches are determined, the event is seeded. Pre-Seeding: swimmers are arranged in heats according to submitted times, usually a day prior to the meet.

Senior Meet—a meet that is for senior level swimmers and is not divided into age groups. Qualification times are usually necessary and will vary depending on the level of the meet.

Senior Nationals—a USA-S National Championship meet for swimmers of any age as long as the qualification times are met.

Session—portion of meet distinctly separated from other portions by locale, time, type of competition, or age group.

Short Course—a 25-yard or 25-meter pool.

Splash—the USA Swimming magazine that is mailed bi-monthly. A benefit of being a member of USA Swimming.

Split—a portion of an event that is shorter than the total distance and is timed (i.e. A swimmer's first 50 time is taken as the swimmer swims the 100 race). It is common to take multiple splits for the longer distances.

Start—the beginning of a race. The dive used to begin a race.

Starter—the official in charge of signaling the beginning of a race and insuring that all swimmers have a fair takeoff.

Stand-up—the command given by the Starter or Referee to release the swimmers from their starting position.

Step-down—the command given by the Starter or Referee to have the swimmers move off the blocks. Usually this command is a good indication everything is not right for the race to start.

Stroke—there are four competitive strokes: butterfly, backstroke, breaststroke, freestyle.

Stroke Judge—the official positioned at the side of the pool, walking the length of the course as the swimmers race. If the Stroke Judge sees something illegal, they report to the referee and the swimmer may be disqualified.

Submitted Time—times used to enter swimmers in meets. These times must have been achieved by the swimmer at previous meets.

Swim-a-Thon—the "fundraiser" trademarked by USA Swimming for local clubs to use to make money.

Swim-off—in a prelims/finals-type competition, a race after the scheduled event to break a tie. The only circumstance that warrants a swim-off is to determine which swimmer makes finals or an alternate, otherwise ties stand.

Swimming World—a paid-subscription swimming magazine.

Taper—the resting phase of a swimmer at the end of the season before the championship meet.

Team Records—the statistics a team keeps, listing the fastest swimmer in the club's history for each age group/ each event.

Timed Finals—competition in which only heats are swum and final placings are determined by those times.

Time Standard—a time set by a meet or LSC or USA-S (etc.) that a swimmer must achieve for qualification or recognition.

Timer—the volunteers sitting behind the starting blocks/ finish end of pool, who are responsible for getting watch times on events and activating the backup buttons for the timing system.

Time Trial—an event or series of events where a swimmer may achieve or better a required time standard.

Top 10—a list of times compiled by the LSC or USA-S that recognizes the top ten swimmers in each single age group (boys and girls) by each event and distance.

Touchpad—the removable plate (on the end of pools) that is connected to an automatic timing system. A swimmer must properly touch the touchpad to register an official time in a race.

Unattached—an athlete member who competes, but does not represent a club or team (abbr. UN).

Unofficial Time—the time displayed on a read out board or read over the intercom by the announcer immediately after the race. After the time has been checked, it will become the official time.

USA-S—the governing body of swimming—USA Swimming.

USA Swimming—the national governing body of the sport headquartered in Colorado Springs.

USA-S ID Number—a sixteen-part number assigned to a swimmer after they have filled out the proper forms and paid their annual dues. The first six parts are numbers of a swimmer's birthdate: Day/Month/Year using zeros as place holders. The next three spaces are the first three letters of the athlete's legal first name. The next letter is the middle initial, followed by the first four letters of the swimmer's last name. For example: USA-S ID# for swimmer Suzanne Eileen Nelson born Aug. 27, 1976 = 082776SUZENELS.

USOTC—United States Olympic Training Center located in Colorado Springs, Colorado.

Warm-down—the recovery swimming a swimmer does after a race when pool space is available.

Warm-up—the practice and "loosening-up" session a swimmer does before the meet or his or her event is swum.

Yards—the measurement of the length of a swimming pool that was built per specs using the American system. A short course yard pool is 25 yards (75 feet) in length.

Yardage—the distance a swimmer races or swims in practice. Total yardage can be calculated for each practice session.

Bibliography

"Able to Stay Golden," Winter 2015, NCAA.org, http://
ncaachampionmagazine.org/features/able-to-stay-golden/
#sthash.3osXOg0J.dpbs, accessed December 20, 2015.

Anderson, Jared, "Missy Franklin Becomes Laureus Ambassador," April
27, 2015, SwimSwam.com, http://swimswam.com/missy-franklin
-becomes-laureus-ambassador/, accessed November 7, 2015.

Anderson, Jared, "Missy Franklin Joins USA Swimming Foundation
as Ambassador," September 24, 2015, SwimSwam.com, http://
swimswam.com/missy-franklin-joins-usa-swimming-foundation
-as-ambassador-video/, accessed November 7, 2015.

Anderson, Jared, "USA Swimming Increasing, But Narrowing,
National Team Athlete Funding in Leadup to Rio," July 13,
2014, Swim Swam.com, http://swimswam.com/usa-swimming
-increasing-narrowing-national-team-athlete-funding-leadup-rio/,
accessed November 9, 2015.

Associated Press, "AP Interview: Olympic Swimmer Missy Franklin
Turns Pro," March 23, 2015, timesfreepress.com, http://www
.timesfreepress.com/news/national/sports/story/2015/mar/23/ap
-interview-olympic-swimmer-missy-franklturn/294801/, accessed
December 20, 2015.

Associated Press, "Injured Missy Franklin Struggles on First Day of
Pan Pacific Championships," last updated August 21, 2014, http://
sports.ndtv.com/swimming/news/228597-injured-missy-franklin
-struggles-on-first-day-of-pan-pacific-championships, accessed
December 20, 2015.

Associate Press, "Michael Phelps Wins 200 Backstroke," May 15, 2015,
ESPN.com, http://espn.go.com/espn/print?id=6554639, accessed
November 9, 2015.

Associated Press, "Missy Franklin (back) Questionable," August 20, 2014,
ESPN.com, http://espn.go.com/espn/print?id=11379437, accessed
December 23, 2015.

Associated Press, "Missy Franklin Overcomes Injury for Fastest Time of the Year," August 3, 2015, *USA Today*, http://www.usatoday.com/story/sports/olympics/2015/08/03/missy-franklin-swimming -injury-backstroke-fina-world-championships/31082031/, accessed November 9, 2015.

Associated Press, "Missy Franklin Shining in Grand Prix Swimming Pool at Orlando," February 8, 2013, *The Denver Post*, http://www .denverpost.com/missyfranklin/ci_22602679/missy-franklin -shining-grand-prix-swimming-pool-at, accessed December 23, 2015.

Associated Press, "Team USA Wins Seventh Straight Duel in the Pool," December 12, 2015, TeauUSA.org, http://www.teamusa.org/News/2015/December/12/Team-USA-Wins-Seventh-Straight-Duel -In-The-Pool, accessed December 30, 2015.

"Athlete Funding for Quad," USA Swimming, http://www. usaswimming.org/_Rainbow/Documents/4c78ec4f-c4da-44aa -b198-96140c856857/Athlete%20Funding%20through%2016%20 FINAL%20Mar.pdf, accessed November 9, 2015.

Auerbach, Nicole, "Teen Missy Franklin Could Swim Seven Events in Olympics," July 1, 2012, http://usatoday30.usatoday.com/sports/olympics/london/swimming/story/2012-07-01/missy-franklin -qualifies-seven-olympic-events/55968250/1#, accessed March 1, 2015.

Auerbach, Nicole, "US Women Set World Record, Win Gold in Medley Relay," August 5, 2012, http://usatoday30.usatoday.com/sports/olympics/london/swimming/story/2012-08-04/usa-womens -medley-relay-sets-world-record-wins-gold/56787496/1, accessed March 3, 2015.

Bonham, Chad, "A Conversation with US. Olympian Missy Franklin," Beliefnet.com http://www.beliefnet.com/columnists/inspiringathletes/2012/06/a-conversation-with-u-s-olympian-missy -franklin.html, accessed February 17, 2015.

Borzi, Pat, "Now at the Pinnacle, an Uneasy Pioneer," July 18, 2012, *The New York Times*, http://www.nytimes.com/2012/07/19/sports/olympics/pinnacle-for-us-swim-coach-teri-mckeever-but-dont-call -her-a-pioneer.html?_r=0, accessed December 31, 2015.

Bowmile, Mitch, "A Look at Missy Franklin's Career Thus Far," April 27, 2015, SwimSwam.com, http://swimswam.com/a-look-at-missy -franklins-career-thus-far/, accessed November 7, 2015.

Bibliography

Bowmile, Mitch, "Missy Franklin takes Down 200m Freestyle US Open Record," December 12, 2015, SwimSwam.com, http://swimswam.com/missy-franklin-takes-down-200m-freestyle-us-open-record/, accessed December 15, 2015.

Braden, Keith, "Sportsnet: Video Shows Missy Franklin in 'Obvious Pain' During Pan Pacs Training," August 19, 2014, SwimSwam.com, http://swimswam.com/sportsnet-video-shows-missy-franklin-obvious-pain-pan-pacs-training-session/, accessed March 1, 2015.

Braden, Keith, "USA vs. Europe to Renew Duel in the Pool Battle in 2015 at IUPUI," February 25, 2015, SwimSwam.com, https://swimswam.com/usa-vs-europe-to-renew-duel-in-the-pool-battle-in-2015-at-iupui/, accessed October 10, 2015.

Brady, Erik, "Olympic Swim Camp: What Happens in Vichy, Stays in Vichy," July 19, 2012, USA Today, http://content.usatoday.com/communities/gameon/post/2012/07/natalie-coughlin-us-swimmers-get-a-kick-out-of-rookies/1#.VkOXcXarTrc, accessed November 7, 2015.

Brian Braiker, "Missy Franklin: The First US Woman to Swim in Seven Events in One Games," July 18, 2012, The Guardian, http://www.theguardian.com/sport/2012/jul/18/missy-franklin-swimming-london-2012, accessed March 1, 2015.

Browning-Blas, Kristen, "Elite Swimmers Hit the Fast Lane on Land Too," October 9, 2009 Denver Post.com, http://www.denverpost.com/lifestyles/ci_13484527, accessed February 13, 2015.

Carroll, Shannon, "Little Miss Sunshine," May 1, 2014, The Daily Californian, http://www.dailycal.org/2014/05/01/little-miss-sunshine-missy-franklin/, accessed February 25, 2015.

Castillo, Mariano and Carter, Chelsea J., "Background of Colorado Shooting Suspect Full of Contrasts," updated July 22, 2012, http://www.cnn.com/2012/07/20/us/colorado-theater-suspect-profile/, accessed March 1, 2015.

CBS/AP, "Swimmer Missy Franklin Dedicates Olympic wins to Colorado," July 31, 2012, http://www.cbsnews.com/news/swimmer-missy-franklin-dedicates-olympic-wins-to-colorado/, accessed March 1, 2015.

Crouse, Karen, "Aiming for the Top, Via the Slow Lane," August 17, 2010, The New York Times, http://www.nytimes.com/2010/08/18/sports/18swimmer.html?_r=0, accessed February 14, 2015.

Crouse, Karen, "Missy Franklin Finds New World on Campus," October 12, 2013, *The New York Times*, http://www.nytimes.com/2013/10/13/sports/golf/missy-franklin-finds-new-world-on-campus.html?_r=0, accessed December 23, 2015.

Crouse, Karen, "Missy Franklin Sheds Her Youth and Embraces a Pro's Challenges," July 31, 2015, *The New York Times*, http://www.nytimes.com/2015/08/02/sports/missy-franklin-sheds-her-youth-and-embraces-a-pros-challenges.html?_r=0.

Crouse, Karen, "Shooting Shakes US Olympic Star," July 20, 2012, http://www.nytimes.com/2012/07/21/sports/olympics/swimming-star-missy-franklin-shaken-by-colorado-shooting.html?_r=0 , accessed March 1, 2015.

Crouse, Karen, "With Grit and a Grin, a Determined Franklin Endures a Painful Test," August 21, 2014, *The New York Times*, http://www.nytimes.com/2014/08/22/sports/a-determined-missy-franklin-endures-a-painful-test.html, accessed December 23, 2015.

Devlin, Neil H., "Missy Franklin Caps Prep Career in Style as Regis Jesuit Take Title," February 13, 2013, *The Denver Post*, http://www.denverpost.com/Sports/ci_22558205/Missy-Franklin-caps-prep-career-in, accessed February 15, 2015.

Drehs, Wayne, "Exceptionally Normal," June 28, 2013, ESPN.com, http://espn.go.com/espnw/news-commentary/article/9432087/olympic-swimmer-missy-franklin-had-ordinary-life-thanks-parents-espn-magazine, accessed December 20, 2015.

Drehs, Wayne, "Franklin Blossoms into Champion" July 2012, ESPN.com, http://espn.go.com/olympics/summer/2012/swimming/story/_/id/8216151/2012-olympics-missy-franklin-blossoms-olympic-champion, accessed February 14, 2015.

Drehs, Wayne, "History in Making? Franklin on Way," July 2, 2012, ESPN.com, http://espn.go.com/olympics/summer/2012/swimming/story/_/id/8120704/2012-summer-olympics-missy-franklin-lives-hype-trials, accessed March 1, 2015.

Drehs, Wayne, "Missy Franklin Reflects on Her 'Insane' Year," December 3, 2012, ESPNW, http://espn.go.com/espnw/news-commentary/article/8677126/olympic-swimmer-missy-franklin-had-surreal-summer-london-espn-magazine-interview-issue, accessed December 22, 2015.

Bibliography

Dube, Rebecca, "Missy Franklin's Dilemma: Go Pro or Go to College?" August 16, 2012, *TODAY Parents*, http://www.today.com/parents/missy-franklins-dilemma-go-pro-or-go-college-946211, accessed December 22, 2015.

Dyer, Dave, "Missy Franklin Wins Two US. Titles at Winter Nationals," December 06, 2015, TeamUSA.org, http://www.teamusa.org/News/2015/December/06/Missy-Franklin-Wins-Two-US-Titles-At-Winter-Nationals, accessed December 15, 2015.

"Exclusive: Missy Franklin: 25 things You Don't Know about Me," August 1, 2012, USmagazine.com, http://www.usmagazine.com/entertainment/news/missy-franklin-25-things-you-dont-know-about-me-201218, accessed February 15, 2015.

Fixler, Kevin. "Missy Franklin: the Next Big Thing in Swimming," July 21, 2011, The PostGame.com, http://www.thepostgame.com/blog/phenom/201107/missy-franklin-next-big-thing-swimming, accessed February 15, 2015.

Forbes Brian, "Regis Freshman Missy Franklin Already World-Class in Swimming," January 14, 2014, *The Denver Post*, http://www.denverpost.com/sportsheadlines/ci_14184459, accessed February 13, 2015.

Ford, Bonnie D., "Coughlin: 'It's Time for Missy'," June 27, 2012, ESPN.com, http://espn.go.com/espn/print?id=8106322, accessed December 21, 2015.

Henderson, John. "Olympic Gold Medalist Missy Franklin Basking in the Spotlight," September 6, 2012, *The Denver Post*, http://www.denverpost.com/ci_21477258/olympic-gold-medalist-missy-franklin-basking-spotlight, accessed December 21, 2015.

Henderson, John, "At long last, London Olympics are here for Regis Jesuit's Missy Franklin," July 28, 2012, *The Denver Post*, http://www.denverpost.com/london2012/ci_21174615/at-long-last-olympics-are-here-missy-frankin, accessed December 21, 2015.

Henderson, John, "Missy Franklin Back in School, Still on National Stage as American Idol," January 28, 2013, *The Denver Post*, http://www.denverpost.com/ci_22458892/missy-franklin-olympic-swimmer-national-stage, accessed December 31, 2015.

Henderson, John, "Missy Franklin Gets First Medal with Bronze in 4x100 Freestyle Relay," July 30, 2012, *The Denver Post*, http://www

.denverpost.com/london2012/ci_21181504/missy-franklin-gets-first
-medal-bronze-4x100-freestyle, accessed December 21, 2015.

Henderson, John, "Missy Franklin Remains on Collegiate Path,
Barring Enormous Endorsement," July 31, 2012, *The Denver Post*,
http://www.denverpost.com/london2012/ci_21200418/missy
-franklin-remains-collegiate-path-mdash-barring-enormous,
accessed December 22, 2012.

Henderson, John, "Missy Franklin Soon to Say Goodbye to Longtime
Swim Coach Todd Schmitz," July 17, 2013, *The Denver Post*, http://
www.denverpost.com/ci_23641697/missy-franklin-soon-say
-goodbye-longtime-swim-coach, accessed December 22, 2015.

Henderson, John, "Missy Franklin Swims High School Meet for First
Time Since Olympic Golds," January 8, 2013, *The Denver Post*,
http://www.denverpost.com/ci_22335684/missy-franklin-high
-school-meet-first-olympic-gold, accessed December 22, 2015.

Henderson, John. "Swimming Phenom Missy Franklin Has Parents
to Thank For Her Success," May 13, 2015, *The Denver Post*. http://
www.denverpost.com/ci_20611983/swimming-phenom-missy
-franklin-has-parents-thank, accessed February 17, 2015.

Henderson, John, "Missy Franklin Wins Sullivan Award as Nation's
Top Amateur Athlete," April 17, 2013, denverpost.com, http://www
.denverpost.com/missyfranklin/ci_23040637/missy-franklin-wins
-sullivan-award-nations-top-amateur, accessed December 22, 2015.

Hendrikson, Brian. "Able to Stay Golden," January 15 2015,
NCAA.org, National Collegiate Athletic Association, http://
ncaachampionmagazine.org/features/able-to-stay-golden/#sthash
.zxjaG2uM.dpbs, accessed February 19, 2015.

Hersey Kathleen, "Call Me Maybe - 2012 USA Olympic
Swimming Team" July 26, 2012, https://www.youtube.com/
watch?v=YPIA7mpm1wU, accessed March 1, 2015.

Hicks, Michael, "Star Power at Regis Jesuit Starts with Frosh Franklin,"
November 30, 2009, *The Denver Post*, https://www.denverpost.com/
colleges/ci_13890918, accessed February 13, 2015.

Hoppes, Lynn, "Missy Franklin Keeps Busy in High School," February
14, 2013, ESPN.com, http://espn.go.com/blog/playbooktrending/
print?id=14215, accessed December 22, 2015.

Isaacson, Melissa, "Elite Athletes Enjoy Competing at High School Level," January 3, 2013, espnW, http://espn.go.com/espnw/news -commentary/olympics/article/8809512/espnw-missy-franklin-elite -athletes-competing-high-school, accessed March 1, 2015.

Jhabvala, Nicki, "Missy Franklin Already Vetting Prospective Brands for Endorsements," Updated July 1, 2015, DenverPost.com, http:// blogs.denverpost.com/olympics/2015/05/25/missy-franklin -already-vetting-prospective-brands-for-endorsements/26960/, accessed, September 21, 2015.

Jhabvala, Nicki, "Missy Franklin Signs First Endorsement Deal, With Speedo," June 18, 2015, DenverPost.com, http://www.denverpost .com/olympics/ci_28339132/missy-franklin-signs-first-endorsement -deal-speedo, accessed, September 21, 2015.

Katz, Michael, "Missy Franklin Doesn't Agree with Justin Bieber's Life Choices," August 5, 2014, SBNation, http://www.sbnation.com/ lookit/2014/8/5/5972549/missy-franklin-doesnt-agree-with-justin -biebers-life-choices, accessed December 23, 2015.

Keith, Braden. "US Olympic Training Camp Begins Saturday in Tennessee," July 6, 2012, SwimSwam.com, http://swimswam.com/ us-olympic-training-camp-begins-saturday-in-tennessee/, accessed November 7, 2015.

Kiszla, Mark, "Mark Kiszla: Missy Franklin's crazy Olympic dream to match Phelps' 22 medals," August 5, 2012, *The Denver Post*, http:// www.denverpost.com/ci_21238534/catch-22-missy-franklin-could -match-michael-phelps, accessed December 22, 2015.

Lanier, Yvette, "Prodigy in the Swimming Pool," June 29, 2008, *The Denver Post*, http://www.denverpost.com/ci_9732643, accessed February 13, 2015.

Linden, Julian, "Olympics – US Swim Team Buoyant after Final Training Camp," July 21 2012, Rueters.com, http:// www.reuters.com/article/2012/07/21/oly-swim-usa-adv -idUSL4E8IL0DR20120721, accessed November 7, 2015.

London 2012: "Missy Franklin Has Body Built for Speed," June 6, 2012, Washington Post, https://www.youtube.com/ watch?v=nkqgJixK1DU, accessed February 25, 2015.

Lord, Craig, "The Wonderful World of Missy Franklin as Laureus Vote Looms," March 13, 2014, SwimVortex.com, http://www

.swimvortex.com/the-wonderful-world-of-missy-franklin-in-her -own-words/, accessed December 30, 2015.

MacMullan, Jackie, "Missy Franklin Wins 200 Backstroke," August 2, 2012, ESPN.com, http://espn.go.com/espn/print?id=8230840, accessed December 22, 2015.

"Mattern Starts Record Run," February 13, 2010, *The Denver Post*, http://www.denverpost.com/sportsheadlines/ci_14393626, accessed February 14, 2015.

McKissick, Lindsey R., "Centennial's Missy Franklin Shocking the Swim World," January 20, 2010, *The Denver Post*, http://www .denverpost.com/ci_17238776, accessed February 13, 2015.

McKissick, Lindsey R., "Missy Franklin Hopes to Join US Olympic Team in 2012," March 4, 2012, *The Denver Post*, http://www .denverpost.com/ci_17373626, accessed February 13, 2015.

McKissick, Lindsey R., "Teen Making Waves in Big Pool," December 12, 2010, *The Denver Post*, http://www.denverpost.com/ci_16837396, accessed February 15, 2015.

Meyer, John, "Missy Franklin to Appear in a Movie Scuba Diving to Help Disabled," December 4, 2012, *The Denver Post*, http://www .denverpost.com/ci_22118069/missy-franklin-appear-movie-scuba -diving-help-disabled, accessed December 22, 2015.

Meyer, John, "World Champion Swimmer Missy Franklin Driving Teammates to Succeed," September 7, 2011, *The Denver Post*, http:// www.denverpost.com/ci_18839901, accessed February 14, 2015.

"Missy Franklin Bio–California Golden Bears–University of California Official Athletic Site, http://www.calbears.com/ViewArticle .dbml?ATCLID=209284219, accessed February 13, 2015.

"Missy Franklin is Top Female Athlete," November 20, 2012, ESPN, http://espn.go.com/olympics/swimming/story/_/id/8654634/ missy-franklin-weighing-whether-swim-high-school, accessed December 22, 2015.

"Missy Franklin, Regis Jesuit," February 21, 2010, *The Denver Post*, http://www.denverpost.com/recommended/ci_14441745, accessed February 13, 2015.

Bibliography

"Missy Franklin Wins 100 Meter Backstroke Gold – London Olympics," July 30, 2015, https://www.youtube.com/watch?v=3nTv7p64pQA, accessed March 3, 2015.

"Missy Franklin: London 2012 Profile," June 26, 2012, NBC Sports, https://www.youtube.com/watch?v=uCT1mG-3kp0&index=10&list=PLJ0XD6JX11yUBS9GggodZY9bnffBY3Vfg, accessed March 1, 2015.

"Missy Franklin at Olympic Games Dedicates Wins to Aurora, Colorado Neighbors," July 31, 2012, ABC News, https://www.youtube.com/watch?v=XJlgmSPrLh8&list=PLJ0XD6JX11yUBS9GggodZY9bnffBY3Vfg&index=106, accessed March 1, 2015.

"Missy Franklin Spreads Cheer among Sick Kids at Children's Hospital," December 14, 2012, *The Denver Post*, http://www.denverpost.com/ci_22189755/missy-franklin-spreads-cheer-among-sick-kids-at, accessed December 30, 2015.

"Missy Franklin Talks about Swimming Through Back 'Discomfort,' Decision to Swim In Finals," August 21, 2014, *Swimming World*, http://www.swimmingworldmagazine.com/news/missy-franklin-talks-about-swimming-through-back-discomfort-decision-to-swim-in-finals/, accessed December 23, 2015.

NCAA, "Champion: Missy Franklin Explains What College Means to Her," January 14 2015, https://www.youtube.com/watch?v=TUvhzdCPEOA&index=107&list=PLJ0XD6JX11yUBS9GggodZY9bnffBY3Vfg, accessed March 1, 2015.

Newberry, Paul, "Franklin Gets Ready to Walk Down High School Aisle," May 15, 2013, AP, http://www.summergames.ap.org/article/franklin-gets-ready-walk-down-high-school-aisle, accessed December 23, 2015.

Olszowy, Lynn, "Missy Franklin's College Career Reaches Bittersweet End," March 18, 2015, ESPNW, http://espn.go.com/espnw/news-commentary/article/12506356/missy-franklin-college-career-reaches-bittersweet-end, accessed December 23, 2015.

Pappas, Stephanie, "Phelps, Lochte & Split-Second Races: How Olympic Timing Tech Works," July 31, 2012, *Live Science*, http://www.livescience.com/21997-phelps-lochte-races-timing-technology.html, accessed November 9, 2015.

ThePostGame Staff, "Justin Bieber Nearly Jeopardizes Missy Franklin's Amateur Status with this Gift," December 5, 2012, ThePostGame, http://www.thepostgame.com/blog/dish/201212/bieber-nearly -jeopardized-missy-franklins-amateur-status, accessed December 22, 2015.

Quinn, Erin, "Swimmer Missy Franklin Responds to Aurora Shooting Tragedy," July 20, 2012, Bleacher Report, http://bleacherreport .com/articles/1266792-usa-olympic-swimming-hopeful-missy -franklin-responds-to-aurora-shooting-tragedy, accessed March 1, 2015.

Race, Loretta. "Missy Franklin Lends Voice to Denver International Airport Welcome Messages," June 17, 2015, SwimSwam.com, http://swimswam.com/missy-franklin-lends-voice-to-denver -international-airport-welcome-messages/, accessed November 7, 2015.

"Regis' Franklin, 15, Wins 200 Freestyle at Grand Prix Meet," November 13, 2010, *The Denver Post*, http://www.denverpost.com/ ci_16600496, accessed February 13, 2015.

"Regis Jesuit's Franklin third in 200 IM," December 3, 2010, https://www.regisjesuit.com/page.aspx?pid=972&storyid3036 =4549&ncs3036=3, *The Denver Post*, accessed February 13, 2015.

Sanchez, "The Golden Girl," June 2012, 5280 – Denver Magazine, http://www.5280.com/magazine/2012/06/golden-girl?page=full accessed February 2015.

Shaikin, Bill, "Missy Franklin Shaken by Colorado Theater Attack," July 26, 2012, http://articles.latimes.com/2012/jul/26/sports/la-sp -oly-swimming-franklin-20120727 , accessed March 1, 2015.

Smith, Michelle, "Franklin Begins Life as College Freshman," August 28, 2013, ESPNW, http://espn.go.com/espnw/news-commentary/ article/9609999/espnw-california-golden-bears-swimmer-missy -franklin-feels-home-berkeley, accessed December 21, 2015.

"Sportswoman of the Year Nominee Missy Franklin Talks to Laureus," March 14, 2014, Laureus.com, https://www.laureus.com/news/ sportswoman-year-nominee-missy-franklin-talks-laureus, accessed December 30, 2015.

Bibliography

Steffen, Jordan, "Olympic Athletes from Colorado Honored by Governor, Fans," August 18, 2012, *The Denver Post*, http://www.denverpost.com/ci_21346606/olympic-athletes-from-colorado-honored-by-governor-fans, accessed December 22, 2015.

Steffen, Jordan, "Servicemen and Women Celebrate Start of Warrior Games," May 11, 2013, *The Denver Post*, http://www.denverpost.com/ci_23224367/servicemen-and-women-celebrate-start-warrior-games, accessed December 23, 2015.

Stump, Scott, "Missy Franklin Reveals Movie Cameo: 'I'm so excited'," August 24, 2012, msn TODAY, http://todayinlondonblog.today.com/_news/2012/08/24/13454903-missy-franklin-reveals-movie-cameo-im-so-excited?lite, accessed December 22, 2015.

"20 Question Tuesday: Missy Franklin," February 1, 2011, *USA Swimming*, http://www.usaswimming.org/ViewNewsArticle.aspx?TabId=1&itemid=3132&mid=8712 accessed February 22, 2015.

"US Sets Record at Duel in the Pool," December 16, 2011, ESPN.com, http://espn.go.com/espn/print?id=7361280 , accessed February 14, 2015

USA Swimming, "Missy Franklin Visits Seacrest Studios at Children's Hospital Colorado," January 6, 2015, sports.NDTV.com, https://www.youtube.com/watch?v=EQuHeD6aXo&list=PLJ0XD6JX11yUBS9GggodZY9bnffBY3Vfg&index=15 , accessed March 1, 2015

USA Swimming, "National Team Bios – Missy Franklin," http://www.usaswimming.org/DesktopDefault.aspx?TabId=1453&Alias=Rainbow&Lang=en&biosid=7418ae3a-418c-4e08-96c7-8b8833106195, accessed February 17, 2015.

USA Swimming, "Time Standards," http://www.usaswimming.org/DesktopDefault.aspx?TabId=1465&Alias=Rainbow&Lang=en, accessed March1, 2015.

Valade, Jodie, "Missy Franklin Has No Regrets about No Decision to Turn Pro," March 18, 2015, *USA TODAY*, http://www.usatoday.com/story/sports/olympics/2015/03/18/missy-franklin-turning-pro-cal-ncaa-meet/24989047/, accessed December 30, 2015.

Vernon, Mike, "Missy Franklin to Leave Cal Swim Team to Focus on Olympics," February 19, 2015, *San Francisco Chronicle*, http://www.sfchronicle.com/collegesports/article/Missy-Franklin-prepares-to-leave-Cal-and-focus-on-6090611.php, accessed February 22, 2015.

"Video: Missy Franklin Talks about Back Injury and Recovery at Pan Pacs," August 21, 2014, SwimmingWorld.com, http://www.swimmingworldmagazine.com/news/video-missy-franklin-talks-about-back-injury-and-recovery-at-pan-pacs/, accessed March 1, 2015.

Warren, Lydia, "It's Missy Mania! How the Teenage Swimmer From a Jesuit High School won America's hearts (and Even aTweet From Justin Bieber) . . . but Refuses to Cash in on her Fame," July 31, 2012, http://www.dailymail.co.uk/news/article-2181589/Missy-Franklin-From-childhood-Olympic-gold.html, accessed March 1, 2015.

"Water Depth and Temperature" *USA Swimming,* http://www.usaswimming.org/ViewMiscArticle.aspx?TabId=1755&mid=7713&ItemId=3551, accessed November 1, 2015.

Woo, Stu, "I Have to Swim Against Her?" January 14, 2013, *The Wall Street Journal,* http://www.wsj.com/articles/SB10001424127887324235104578241961511333962, accessed December 22, 2015.

Wright, David, "Gold Medalist Missy Franklin Competes in High School," January 9, 2013, ABC News report, https://www.youtube.com/watch?v=4VjzuWaQHII, accessed March 5, 2015.

Zaccardi, Nick, "Missy Franklin Embrace 'Disappointments' Going into Olympic Season," November 12, 2015, NBCSports, http://olympics.nbcsports.com/2015/11/12/missy-franklin-minneapolis-swimming/, accessed December 15, 2015.

Zaccardi, Nick, "Missy Franklin Returns to Winning Ways in Minneapolis," November 13, 2015, NBCSports, http://olympics.nbcsports.com/2015/11/13/missy-franklin-michael-phelps-katie-ledecky-ryan-lochte-minneapolis-swimming-friday/, accessed December 15, 2015

For more information visit
nataliedavismiller.com

Other books in the
ZonderKidz Biography series

Speed to Glory:
The Cullen Jones Story

Natalie Davis Miller

He conquered the thing that nearly took his life. At five years old, Cullen Jones nearly drowned. While some people might stay away from water after that, Jones conquered his fear when his mother enrolled him in a swimming class. Not only did he learn to swim, he quickly found that he was a good swimmer ... and would become one of the world's best. Discover how faith, courage, and hard work led Jones to win an Olympic gold medal and set a new world record in his event. Find out what can happen when you overcome fear and strive to become all God calls you to be. Includes a personal note from Cullen Jones.

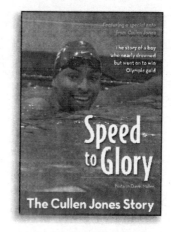

Available in stores and online!

CPSIA information can be obtained at www.ICGtesting.com
Printed in the USA
LVOW07s2019200816

501159LV00006B/11/P